*Heart's Oratorio*

# Heart's Oratorio

One Woman's Journey
through Love, Death, and Modern Medicine

Mary Oak

GOLDENSTONE PRESS | *Benson, North Carolina*

Published by Goldenstone Press
P.O. Box 7
Benson, North Carolina 27504
www.goldenstonepress.com

ISBN: 978-0-9832261-8-5

Cover artwork: Adam McLean, *The Soul, personified as a woman,
contemplates its heart.* This oil painting is McLean's version of an image from
a late fifteenth century Flemish illuminated manuscript.

Cover and book design: Eva Leong Casey/Lee Nichol

Printed in the USA

# GOLDENSTONE PRESS

GOLDENSTONE PRESS seeks to make original spiritual thought available as a
force of individual, cultural, and world revitalization. The press is an integral
dimension of the work of the School of Spiritual Psychology. The mission of the
School includes restoring the book as a way of inner transformation and awakening to spirit. We recognize that secondary thought and the reduction of books
to sources of information and entertainment as the dominant meaning of reading places in jeopardy the unique character of writing as a vessel of the human
spirit. We feel that the continuing emphasis of such a narrowing of what books
are intended to be needs to be balanced by writing, editing, and publishing
that emphasizes the act of reading as entering into a magical, even miraculous
spiritual realm that stimulates the imagination and makes possible discerning
reality from illusion in the world. The editorial board of Goldenstone Press is
committed to fostering authors with the capacity of creative spiritual imagination who write in forms that bring readers into deep engagement with an inner
transformative process rather than being spectators to someone's speculations. A
complete catalogue of all our books may be found at *www.goldenstonepress.com.*
The web page for the School of Spiritual Psychology is *www.spiritualschool.org.*

10 9 8 7 6 5 4 3 2 1

Dedicated to
Gaia Sophia, Earth Wisdom

# Table of Contents

ORATORIO: a choral composition
for orchestra and voices, typically on a sacred theme,
derived from ORATORY: a small chapel or shrine

☙

*The voices of the heart can be wept, can be garbled,*
*can be whispered, called out, sung.*
*Fade into the eternal ink of night's silence*
*Ring again with bravado of sun,*
*Are tremulous, praising, halting, poised.*

To begin:

Silence, out of which all words emerge

*September, 2007*
*Humble, Texas*

## Hades Transit

Slipping out of coma, wresting erasure, I enter stuttering awareness. The last thing I clearly remember is standstill. My fiancé David and I at the very back of the airplane. Late. Worried that we
may not make our connecting flight. Enclosed space, forced air,
standing in the last row. The clatter of overhead bins opening.
Fellow passengers reaching for their baggage. Unheeded requests
from the flight attendants to allow those with connecting flights to
disembark first. Standing still, the weight of my overloaded back-
pack, its straps digging into my shoulders. The press of people into
the aisle, people and their bags ahead of us. Delay.

    The next thing I know:

… blear and blur—*black pulsating void dissolving* as I am drawn into the sounds surrounding me, low tomes of conversation     *I follow the silver thread, my link*     the push and squeeze of breath—my body propped up in bed, my throat on fire, something filling my mouth pushing air     my lids slowly lifting *if I close my eyes I may be absorbed back into nothingness* opening wide, I slowly look around to find David reaching out and welcoming me back, his dear voice telling me I made it.

Does he know where I have been? Do I?

If I was a master of meditative states, perhaps I could name the realms I am returning from. If I was a shaman, perhaps I'd have words. But I am just an ordinary woman made extraordinary by having survived. Hesiod articulated it best: Imagine an egg, absolutely empty. Then take away the shell. It's there that I am returning from. Back to the shell of my body from dancing in oblivion.

my throat is raw     *if I close my eyes I may be there again, dissolved into nameless terrain the sheer enormity of limitlessness that could swallow me*     no, no, if I wriggle my fingers I can feel my body even as I don't quite trust gravity     *dizziness swells as I rise the stars are infinite searing through*     no, no if I squeeze David's hand     hold on     can I stay but     I can't say anything     my throat is burning     *the stars throb, scintillating*     clutch     *out of dimness into light*     my mouth is filled with hard plastic worse than the dentist's     *out of lightness into density*     I can't say anything can't ask where *how easily I could unhitch*     No, no I am here  *meeting destiny*

Over the next few days, having moved out of two days of unconsciousness, the story of time I have lost is stitched together.

Gossamer thread. Durable thread. The night before we left for Paris, I dreamt that we flew south from Seattle into a hurricane. I didn't realize it would be my own fierce weather.

I am here with David. He is here with me. *I am.* We are here. I am alive. We are here in the hospital. We were on our way from our Seattle home to Paris, yet now we are in the hospital. We are in light and sound and curiosity. *I am.* Alive, groggy and intubated. We are in the intensive care unit of Kingwood Medical Center in—of all places—Humble, Texas. David has filled in the blanks for me: A few days ago, our connecting flight to Paris was late. They were paging us for final boarding. We were rushing. I told David to run on ahead. He was a hundred feet or so down the hall. I collapsed.

My heart stopped. Resuscitation kept me alive.

David stayed beside me the first twenty-four hours. He dealt with the doctors. He tried to tell them that I had "Athlete's Heart," the genetic heart defect known to hit basketball players without any warning, and how I had been asymptomatic for years. He kept vigil—my lifeline, my gravity, mission control for journey into the beyond, and back. He dozed off a bit in the padded chair next to my bed. On the second evening my brother, Niles, flew in from San Francisco. I was still unconscious. They knew that the odds were against my memory being recovered. David and Niles got a motel near the hospital and slept. On the third day, I awoke. Somehow, I knew where I was. Or I've forgotten that I forgot. The nursing team talked to me the whole time I was unconscious.

Tentatively, I stand. The polished floor of the hospital room is cool under my feet. I hold up my new brown camisole. A clean cut runs from top to bottom. My bra has been sliced apart in the front, too. This slashing is my own *kriah*, the Jewish rending of one's clothes when a loved one dies, in recognition that the fabric of one's being will never be the same. I hold the ruined clothing in my hands, wondering: Can it be mended?

This is my first time standing and I am already tired. I put the ripped clothing back in my bag, next to the pad of paper with my notes and return to sink into the bed. When I came to, the tube that was breathing me wouldn't allow for me to speak. David was there, with my glasses and paper and pen. I wrote notes to him. My scribbles remain without his spoken responses. Clearly he had to go over things again and again—an anaphora of coming to. For ten pages I alternate between "Ice!" ... "I'm so sorry!" ... "hurts" ... "I need to pee" and huge scrawlings of "I love you!" Towards the end, I stopped repeating myself: "How are you?"... "endurance" ... "pray with me" ... "remedies" ... "this is surreal."

My "private" room is drab in its high-tech sterility. I've spent a lot of time gazing out the generous window, observing the lofty and ever-changing clouds above the whiz and zoom of the freeway. I had a visceral response when we made the reservation, in order to save five hundred bucks by flying via Houston. I didn't want to go there. Little do I know that it will cost well over fifty thousand dollars for this visit! I watch the clouds, finding consolation in knowing that this landscape inspired Georgia O'Keefe when she first came west. I vow to live to learn their names; to differentiate between them: nimbus ... cirrus ... cumulus ... stratocumulus.

I have been in hospitals before, but never admitted as a patient. Now I get center stage—the bed—surrounded by beige: the walls, the sink, the curtain between the door and the bed—a blare in fluorescence. An unremarkable backdrop to a team of kind and caring nurses, whom David has already befriended by the time I am awake. The first one I meet is Renee, and I like that her name means "reborn." She works seven shifts of fourteen hours a month and has six-year-old quadruplets at home. There is cheerful Aimee, more subdued Mildred, and an aide, Lewin, from Kenya, who lights up when he takes my blood pressure at three in the morning. I mention Wangari Maathai, and her tree-planting work decades ago. They change the sheets, they change the IV's.

*bivalirudin / adenosine / Midazolam hcl / amiodorone / propafol / etomidate / lidocaine / amiodorone / diphenhydramine / metropropol tartate / diphenhydramine / amiodorone / morphine / kcl / pantoprazazole / sod chl / amiodorone / verapamil / magnesium sulfate / potassium chloride / amiodorone / succinylcholine / heparin sodium / dextrose / nitroglycerin / D5% / amiodorone / locm / sore throat spray / amiodorone*

David and Niles have remained constant throughout. They've made phone calls to my seventeen-year-old daughter staying with a friend, my three grown sons in their respective homes, to my dad, to close friends. They've kept track of the care I am being given. They've told me what is going on slowly enough for me to comprehend it in my twilight state. They've filled me in on consultations and conversations I've missed during my induced coma. Niles, my little brother—no longer littler. Besides being six feet tall, he is a big help. I am so grateful that he has been here to spell David. He is on my team, willing to be another set of ears. With his irrepressible humor, he's made jokes that I found amusing and then forgot, before I finished laughing.

*12 hours of Oxygen / 1 sensor 02 oximax / 1 IV Cath Prot+ / 1 left heart kit merit / 1 syringe medrad inj / 3 cath angio 6F / 1 dressing tegaderm / 3 venipucture / 2 xr chest / 1 CT head-brain w/o contras / 1 CT scan c-SPINE w/o cont / 1 ct scan pelvis w/o cont / 4 arterial punctures / 1 vent mgmt initial day / 1 vent mgmt subsequent d / 3 echocariograms / 1 inj coronary angiogram. 1 inj lt angio / 1 cath heart lt perc ret / 1 s&I ventricular / art a / 1 S&I pul/ang/aor/co / 3 ECG tracing*

When I first came to, through tubes and above my neck brace, David soothed me by stroking my face, the only place he could reach through all I was hooked up to. Joking, he told me, "I'm so glad you weren't there during your arrest." Then his eyes filled up and he whispered, "I almost lost you." Flooded with remorse, with gratitude, I reached out to clasp his familiar hand as best I could. He brought me the yogurt I like for breakfast, knowing the hospital food doesn't appeal to me. Niles tracked down a remedy that was prescribed to David over the phone, "to clear the death forces."

In that clearing, I write haiku:

> *Intravenous tubes*
> *hanging every which a-way*
> *who figured this out?*

I rest and rest some more, after journeying so close to obliteration and oblivion. Doctors come to see me. They position themselves at the foot of the bed, far away from me. I can easily see they are concerned, tense. They insist that a defibrillator be implanted here and now. I am not ready. I understand that this cardiac team does not specialize in my heart defect: hypertrophic cardiomyopathy (HCM). I just want to go home to weigh out the choices. I refuse to be rushed into anything. Niles and David support me in this, doubly advocating for me. The doctors warn us that leaving without the safety net of having my own defibrillator is ill-advised. When I will not budge, they surrender, in a shrugging-their-shoulders kind of way. I am drugged up with a hefty dose of Amiodorone, a heavy-duty antiarrhythmic drug to prevent ventricular fibrillation, so I can make the trip home.

I rest into the mantle of prayer that enfolds me, issuing from a score of hearts that hold me close at this time. No tatters in this fabric of grace.

∽❧

*September, 2007*
*Houston*

## Airborne

It's my first time in a wheelchair, my feet pressed firmly into the footrests. I've been holding our carry-on bag since David pushed me through check-in and security. Steel beams curved and bent, spacious glass: George Bush Intercontinental Airport, Houston. We are waiting on standby for a plane back to Seattle. Not quite the trip we had in mind. Not quite what most couples deal with in their days of devotion and swoon.

David comes back from the airline counter with a chunky, copper-bearded middle-aged man, whose tan face is beaming. David gestures towards me as they approach. "This is Mary." As if I am a celebrity, the stranger takes my hand: "I'm Bobby Todd and I just wanted to meet you. I overheard your husband talking about your situation. You look fantastic!"

David adds, "Bobby's an EMT ... "

"Have been for twenty-five years, and before that an army

medic. I've never seen a case like yours; it makes my work worth-
while." He goes off to find his wife, Michelle, who is also an emergency medic. She is equally enthusiastic about me. "Miracle," "remarkable," "lucky" are all stressed.

We are not far from where I collapsed four days ago. David
wheels me over to the spot nearby Gate 21. Sunlight is streaming
down on a gleaming white floor from high vaulted windows. No
trace of disaster or grace in this shrine to aviation.

I stand in the place where I almost died. "Do you remember
anything?" David asks. We hoped I might recollect something in
returning here, but my mind is vacant. I shake my head, "Nothing." Did I have any warning signs? Which direction did I fall in?
How did my heart feel? Weak from standing, I sit back down in
the wheelchair, parked by this gateway that could have been my
final exit. David tells me the story again:

"I ran ahead to the ticket counter," he points to a gate at the
end of the hall. "I heard you cry out, and then there was a kind of
group moan. I turned back and people were gathering. I didn't see
they were around you until I got back here. You were lying here." I
simply don't remember. He describes how three people knelt down
around me: a surgical nurse, a doctor, and an EMT who took
charge as he began chest compressions. The nurse did mouth-to-
mouth. David points to the floor as if I were lying there. "The doctor was on your right. He checked out your ankle, wrist, neck, and
kept saying, 'I can't find a pulse.' I held your left hand and said,
'Come on back, Mary. Come on, breathe,' over and over again."

From whatever void I slipped into there as my body lay
prone on the polished floor, David's touch provided an anchor, a
lifeline. From wherever I might have been, hovering above, I must

have heard his entreaty. He provided the needed gravity for me to return to earth. From the calm expansiveness of where we let go, I insisted on holding on for dear life, a dear life with him. I squeeze his hand as he continues. He tells me how a crowd—maybe a hundred—were gathered around the circle of people doing the CPR, just watching.

"You started to gasp. The doctor was saying, 'It sounds as if she's trying to breathe.' The EMT in charge said, 'No, that is agonal breathing.'" David chokes up, "I didn't know exactly what that meant, but I knew they meant you were dying. You were going like this … " He imitates gasping desperately.

He tells me how for a moment he thought he'd be one of those people whose fiancée dies, but that only lasted a moment. There was so much going on. "The nurse stopped the mouth-to-mouth and handed the EMT a flashlight to check out your pupils. They were seeing if you were brain-dead. You weren't, so they continued the CPR."

David takes a deep breath. Is this dramatic story he is recounting really mine? The airport personnel arrived with their defibrillator, and the man who brought it tried to follow the directions, but it didn't work. How they fetched a second one, and this time it functioned properly and delivered a shock, but it didn't start my heart.

"Just then, a swarm of firefighters rushed in."

"How many?" I ask.

"There were two trucks—eight firemen. All men. They cleared the crowd. A fireman knelt down in front of you, gave one look at the defibrillator and said, 'Get rid of this toy!' He tossed it aside and got their sturdier defibrillator ready."

I smile, appreciating that David would, of course, notice the tools. "Then one of them began asking me a bunch of questions. It was all surreal. I was in a daze." I'm still dazed, but he remembers clearly—a restraining collar, oxygen. My electrician sweetheart describes how the voltage was so strong that everyone had to move away when the shocks were delivered. How they began with a hundred millivolts, then two hundred, then three hundred—to no avail. But finally, when it was stepped up to four hundred and fifty millivolts, my pulse returned.

I listen carefully, wondering if anything that took place here will come back into my awareness.

He goes on, "Then the EMT who did the CPR shook my hand and wished me luck. He had to catch a plane. I didn't even get his name—I just thanked him. It all happened so fast; he was in a hurry." He describes a big man, stocky, dark, in his forties with short hair.

I sigh. "I can't even thank him, or the others. They won't even know that I survived!" Gratitude streams between us for these unknown saviors. I squeeze his hand again. "Okay, go on ..."

"Well, the shock worked, and you were moaning, and began to thrash about, flailing your arms. You were fighting them as they put you on the stretcher. Poor girl ... ," he pauses in tenderness, "you didn't understand, they were trying to help. And boy, are you strong!" He laughs. I take it as a compliment. (Later, I will read the Emergency Physician Record for Cardiopulmonary Resuscitation, which says about me, "Patient not following any commands, agitated, thrashing about, combative, incoherent, pupils dilated.")

He tells how he came with me to the ambulance and then, instead of taking off right away, they did a couple of cardioversions there, more shocks to stabilize my heart (how many shocks is that? ... not that I am counting). And how we finally raced off to the hospital.

I shrug, perplexed at my mind's erasure. My conscious memories of this event are completely obliterated, but what happened here is lodged in my body, indelible. I will need to return to the sudden death embedded in my flesh in order to eventually release its terror.

But for now, David wheels me to the plane, and gingerly I walk down the aisle. We both have middle seats and no one is willing to trade with us. So I sit between two women who, along with a lot of other things, remain indistinct to me. The plane taxis down the runway, and I feel the lift and jolt as we become airborne. After awhile, images flicker on the plane's movie screen that hangs above and ahead of us. When I crane my neck around, I can see David across the aisle in the row behind me, watching *The Fantastic Four*. I've chosen to read instead, finding the place in my book—*Root Memories*—where I left off five days ago, the pages surprisingly unruffled.

I glance up from time to time to see amazing feats of special powers on the screen, but animated heroics fall short of all that saved me: from David's steady presence, to Niles dropping everything to be with me, to the passersby who resuscitated me, to all the medical high-tech contraptions that kept me alive. I wonder what my heart makes of this velocity that set it so askew just days ago, this acceleration that outpaces time. Out the window on the other side of the woman to my right, I can see the blanketed sky, pearly white. But this earthbound altitude is low, compared to the heights where I've recently traveled. This muffled flight resembles the blank expansiveness I retain in erasure, yet sense a potent presence, just beyond.

∽

*2007, 1975, and 1997*
*Seattle and Chartres*

## New Mysteries

My unexpected turn of cardiac arrest prevented a visit to Chartres Cathedral, a destination that I held dear. I had been there twice before. At seventeen, I sat in the center of the labyrinth and ate a pomegranate—my communion with a mother goddess older than cathedral stones. The next morning, I made my way through the sleepy town to the cathedral at dawn. There I discovered a side door to the crypt, open and beckoning. I entered. Past a few chapels, I found an open gate and another set of steps down into an ancient grotto. For over an hour, I sat in reverie by the Druidic well, sacred to the goddess. Purity streamed up from the ground, wisdom, a crystalline presence. I prayed, "Goddess of deep springs, who quenches all thirst, may I walk in your way."

For centuries, young women came there to receive blessings for fertility and motherhood—first from a Druidic pregnant goddess, succeeded by Our Lady. Within a few months of my prayer of dedication in that place, I met my future first husband, Atum, and within three years became a mother myself.

∽

Twenty-two years and four children later, growing towards the other end: to queen, to crone, I returned in pilgrimage to Chartres. Unaccustomed with taking time to myself, I traveled alone by train. As I arrived, the bells were pealing. I walked from the train station though the medieval town to come to stand before her face so worn, so familiar and yet new to me. Chartres Cathedral. The stone was darker than I recalled, a slate sky behind the copper green roof and spires. There was so much to take in, stories inscribed in stone: prophets, apostles, great teachers, guardians. How many hands placed and carved the stones, erected the columns, secured the doors? I paused before entering, tears streaming in gratitude to have returned.

Over the main door, Christ was still seated surrounded by the four *hioth*: eagle, bull, angel, man, with many other beings arcing over. I entered to high mass: hand-held bells ringing, the Kyrie, seven priests giving communion. I turned, lifting my gaze, to behold the spherical rose window above the western doors. Twelve petals unfolded in a luminous wheel. Astonishing hues of lapis and ruby shone down on another rose, the center of the labyrinth paved into the floor. The unicursal path with its many windings was concealed by chairs, with only the center revealed, framed by the straight lines of the aisle. I wanted to clear the pews away, indignant to find people walking over that sacred center in total disregard.

I moved away from the obscured labyrinth and came to our Lady of the Pillar, a Black Madonna draped in lace, ornate and sparkling, her dark son emerging from the folds of her gown. Many candles flickered at her shrine: stands of tapers, ruby votives. Flowers lay before her: pink roses lush against cold stone. A garland of golden hearts was strung above her: the immaculate heart of Mary, each heart a different design, a different aspect. One pierced, another aflame, another abloom with lily.

Underneath my identity as a modern American woman pondering signs and traces, there was a memory that guided me, invoked by that consecrated place. No crucifix. Behind the central altar, in white marble, Mary ascended, surrounded by angels. The relic enshrined there was worn by the Holy Mother they say, during the birth of the Christ child. Her mantle—the Sancta Camisia, her veil. But is not this whole cathedral her veil?

After circumambulating within and without, waiting for the crypt to open, I descended. I followed a tour to the ancient grotto. I discovered the gate left open. Alone again at the earliest foundation, I lingered surrounded by deep silence and ruggedly hewn lime stone. The silence followed me, a consecration. Later, I learned of an ancient rite that was performed here, echoing the mysteries of Eleusis. Every fall, the Black Virgin was carried to the subterranean grotto, to remain there until spring. Persephone's descent.

~~⌒

Ten years later, at forty-nine, in preparing to return to Chartres as part of our pre-wedding trip to Paris, I learned of the major mystery school that flourished at Chartres for two hundred years, between 1000 and 1200. The masters who resided there were influenced by Platonic ideals and a cosmic understanding of the Christ being. Pupils spent years mastering the seven liberal arts, which required discipline and a strong inner life. The teachings (that are more or less lost to us) emphasized spirit in matter, microcosm reflecting macrocosm through Natura, nature known as a living being. The work of these masters was eventually found heretical by the church and silenced. Nevertheless, the cathedral remained a place of transformation, and after long journeys, pilgrims slept there to receive healing.

Mystery school, masters, memories of grace. Seized with eagerness to go on this trip, I was happy to be on the way to Chartres once again to pay homage to the ancient school. I wanted to feel the power of centuries of devotion and fall into reverie as I had before. But it was not to be. The space-age arches of the airport in Houston, ground control to outer space travel, was as cathedralic as it got.

I hadn't counted on encountering another form of mystery, invisible but on the same hand, as potent as what resided in the old initiations. I had often reflected on Rudolf Steiner's understanding that as humanity's consciousness has evolved, we have shifted away from spiritual initiations being a prescribed path, given by a teacher, only for chosen ones. In our time, there is no need to retreat from life; but that initiations are undergone through karmic relationship. Life becomes the altar; we become the temple for one another, human encounter the sacrament. This sacred space is no longer a cathedral of stone, but the community that weaves through hearts across distances of time and space, creating a new temple.

After my collapse, as I drifted between stupor and waking, I was aware of an emanation of love from those who held me in their prayers. My son Emmanuel, twenty-five now, had never overtly demonstrated any kind of spiritual inclinations. In an expository piece on MySpace he wrote, "I view love as warm, giving, and sharing. My association with love is life. This was recently reinforced when my mom was in the hospital sedated and I didn't know what condition she would be in, if and when she recovered. I firmly believe the power of love played a prominent role in my mom's recovery. I, like many other people I know, sent heartfelt love to her. I find it more than a coincidence that my heart became warm and full with life as it reverberated with love being sent her way. The next day there was a significant improvement in her condition, beyond what doctors and obviously we could have hoped for in a best case scenario."

This was a new glory, to find in returning from my descent to the nether worlds, that I could rest in the presence of tangible prayer. I revered this as once I had paid homage to an ancient well. A new discovery of sacredness: my pierced heart, returning to life aflame with love radiating to me from fellow pilgrims, the sweet-scented lily of their intention taking firm root with its pure bloom.

∽��∾

*Late September, 2007*
*Seattle*

## Cardiac Consultation: What to Do?

Early autumn and we're back home in Seattle. David and I sit at one of our favorite places at Green Lake, what we've come to call "Oak Knoll," a circle of twelve oak trees on a hill that overlooks the lake. The lanes that encircle the expanse of water are crowded with walkers, many leashed to their dogs, joggers, roller-bladers, an occasional biker. We sit still, remembering that not long ago someone told us that she calls this popular city park "Sacred Lake" because of all the circumambulations that take place, all the conversations that linger like prayers. Leaves are changing from green to gold and this year is redder than usual. I am weeping again, hoping to take a cue from the trees around me.

A lot to let go of, and tears come easily, flow without warning: there is the trauma of my cardiac arrest and twenty-four hours of being on a respirator, the heavy sedations. Whimpers arise from me when I start to fall asleep. The whole inside of my right thigh is dark purple, bruised from the cardiac catheter (for a procedure I didn't even need that caused complications and cost thousands of dollars!). There is my resistance to becoming a bionic woman; high tech has never been my thing, and to think of a machine set in my chest and wired to my heart gives me the creeps.

My ten days since returning to Seattle have settled into a pattern: rest, walking, an energetically nourishing bath, more rest, and researching options or various consultations in between.

The big question is: What to do now so I don't suffer another cardiac arrest? Everything points to implanting a defibrillator (an ICD—Implantable Cardiac Defibrillator). Dr. Stout, the cardiologist who originally recommended this intervention two years ago, doesn't say, "I told you so," although she would be justified to do so. She compassionately reiterates the need for this device to protect me. "This is a mourning process for you, not a walk in the park." Dr. Lutack, the naturopath whose expertise is cardiology and is conservative about medical intervention, is in complete agreement. It is also strongly urged by Lisa Salberg, the founder/director of the Hypertrophic Cardiomyopathy Association (HCMA) who is very matter-of-fact about having one herself, as does her daughter, as a precaution. Her sister died from sudden death of HCM and she's been helping people like me ever since.

I still have burn marks on my chest from where paddles were placed to deliver the jolts that stimulated my heart to beat again. An ICD is a miniature version of this same technology that saved my life. I want to make peace with this crowning glory of technological achievement, but I bristle to think of such a mechanism becoming a part of my anatomy. What an opportunity to embrace what I would never have accepted in the past. I find it comforting to discover that an Amish family of five with HCM elected to have ICDs implanted. Nothing like sudden death to invite a different perspective.

During my hospital stay in Humble, I chose not to be motivated by fear, and I remain steadfast to that commitment. Over and over I am told that I am a walking miracle. The statistics are sobering: the success rate of resuscitating people with cardiac arrest is only 2–5% outside of the hospital. Only 10% of those who survive aren't brain damaged. I am told that I am still at high risk for recurrence, or as Lisa Salberg says, "You're a china doll right now." She also tells me that one of the drugs I am on, Amiodorone, "is a good med, if it doesn't kill you first."

We meet with Dr. W, an electrophysiologist who was recommended by Dr. Lutack for being conservative in his approach. I have dreamt of him as a being of light, and now it's time to meet him. I am armed with our questions: How often do infections occur? How often does an ICD misfire? How often does the battery need to be changed? After David and I wait in the exam room for almost half an hour, the doctor breezes in, almost breathless. Tan and lanky, he has sandy gray hair, slightly balding. Gold-framed reading glasses rest far down his nose. He has my file in his hand and after amiable introductions, he shares his marvel at my luck in surviving. Then he settles into being grave.

In a distinct voice, warm yet authoritative, he asks if we have any idea how extreme the pressures in my heart are. "Off the charts. I have never seen them this high. A pressure like that overstrains the heart. You shouldn't be walking around with it." He takes time to make a sketch and explain about the imbalance due to high demand, a limited flow that causes obstruction; an inadequate supply/demand ratio at the source of my circulation.

Furthermore, he tells us, "Hypertrophs need to be approached carefully. They are notoriously tough." He warns that without being repaired first, my heart would be at high risk for an ICD to actually work. We talk over the fixes: either alcohol ablation of the septum, which he sees as imprecise as throwing a bomb in and hoping for a good result; or septal myectomy, where some of the enlarged septal muscle is actually shaved off. There is an urgency in his voice as he says that something has to be done, and soon. Thankfully, he lowers the dose of Amiodorone, exclaiming, "You don't want to be on that! It may be effective in reducing dysrhythmias, but it is one of the most potent and toxic drugs there is."

In the next few days I will research and weigh out the choices: septal myectomy, septal ablation, an ICD. Or I could choose no interventions at all and adjust my life to that, with debilitating drugs or none at all. I have a consultation on the phone with Dr. Incao, an Anthroposophical doctor who has helped me in the past. Much to my surprise, he recommends the surgery. He sees my collapse in a place where help was readily available as a serious warning. Like so many others have pointed out, I must have work to do and I need to ensure that I stay around to do it. Because I know that Dr. Incao's main focus is on the energetic level of healing, I have enormous respect for his perspective: that at times intervention on a mechanistic level is necessary, that it will actually help bring about a change in my subtle bodies. I am all for that! Nothing he says is new to me: to let go of attachment, to trust the spiritual worlds, to embrace the opportunity to take initiative, to keep questioning why this has happened to me, to offer it up to the angels, to be courageous as I go into this extreme of mechanism. But somehow in his counsel, truth has become vital and breathing—no longer a concept, but felt grace.

As we look towards choosing surgery, David takes me to walk by Puget Sound at Golden Gardens. The sun lowers over the mountains, throwing long shadows as we walk along the familiar shore. We are both somewhat stunned and need the expansiveness of the beach to intervene. We walk holding hands; each of us sigh from time to time and share our consternation. Considering getting the ICD was itself a stretch, and now?

❧

*Early October, 2007*
*Seattle*

## Cardiac Consultation II: Scarlet

It is a Friday afternoon and the Cardiothoracic Surgery Clinic is eerily empty except for us. We've come to interview a possible surgeon, Dr. V, who has a high reputation in this area for being experienced and skilled in performing septal myectomies, which seems to be the gold standard fix for my overly-strained heart. I know that even though our questions matter, in the end, I will choose him—or not—based on our impressions of him, not his credentials. Only meeting him will decide it.

He enters and after shaking our hands, sits down across from us, framed by a wall of cardiology texts on the bookcase behind him. He looks to be in his fifties, gray hair combed back from his high forehead. He has piercing blue eyes and wears a milk white coat with his name stitched in red thread. I want to check out his hands, considering they may be inside of me in a way no one has ever been, but they are hidden under the desk. Before we have time to tell our story, he tells us that Dr. Stout has filled him in and he has looked through my file. He reassures us that the operation will reduce my chance of arrhythmias and sudden death, that it is the right thing to do for my heart. He says that since my heart has generalized hypertrophy of the left ventricle, it elevates the pressures and that the surgery can change that. This is measured in milliliters of mercury, and is currently one hundred and eighty-five to two hundred and ninety-two. Zero is normal; mine could be reduced to twenty after the myectomy. He relaxes in his chair and takes time to be with us and answer each question that we have, patiently.

His voice gentle yet firm, he tells us that he has done this operation many times and has a hundred percent success rate; that it involves cutting a trough in the left ventricle that would be one to two centimeters wide, and one centimeter deep. He tells us this can be done through the aortic valve, using special instruments. He informs us that the surgery should take three or four hours, that I will need to be in the intensive care unit for a couple of days, that I will be monitored for a few more days after that. We speak of the necessity of the ICD. He can put leads in during the surgery and then Dr. W can implant it after six or seven days of my hospitalization.

At this point, a tall thin woman rushes in, introducing herself as Mary Scarlett. I immediately notice that "scar" is in her name, along with the color of blood. She is a specialized nurse practitioner, Dr. V's assistant. I have the sense that she is tense, as she stands beside the desk, perched on high heels. A heavy necklace of agates with their melancholy colors peeks through her open white coat. I will learn that she often seems as if she is running between places because there is so much for her to cover, and the intensity that burns through her is of vigilance.

Dr. V resumes, coming now to the risks: of bleeding, infection, stroke, valve injury, death. He warns that my mitral valve may possibly need to be replaced, depending on the amount of obstruction, but that can't be determined until "we get in there." At one point, he laughs and we join in—startled by a cat scurrying outside, between ferns that grow on the bank rising up beside the large, low window. He makes it clear that we need to act soon. As an aside, he suggests that I may be a good candidate for a heart transplant. This is so far-fetched I can't even write it down in my flurry of notes. But I can't forget this ominous suggestion.

Dr. V shakes our hands again, firmly, taking leave. Mary Scarlett, who has caught her breath by now, lingers and talks to us about scheduling. She emphasizes that we need to take care of this soon. Next Thursday at 7:30 a.m. there's an opening for me, here at Northwest Hospital. There are papers to sign. David and I look at each other: have we chosen this? I am not sure when in this hour I decided, but I have, and I can tell that David is in agreement. I fill out the forms. Seven days to prepare for break and entry.

☙

*Fall, 2007*
*Seattle*

## Circle of Allies

The year begins to contract as the autumnal equinox passes and the days are shrinking. We come to Michaelmas. Each year at this time, I contemplate who this archangelic being is and understand more of his loving warrior energy. My sense of him began when I was thirteen or so, during frequent walks in the Wissahickon woods. Not far from where Rosicrucians had created a hermitage in the late sixteen hundreds, I discovered an ash tree struck by lightning, lying across a forgotten path. I called it "The Place of Archangel Michael." I knew solace there. Was it his presence or the echo of lightning? Strength flowed into me in that secret place that I sought out over the years. I would sit on the fallen tree and watch its bark peel off, revealing smooth blond wood that eventually darkened and deteriorated.

I grasp hold of images of courage: Michael with his sword arm raised, Padma Dakini with a hook-knife to cut through illusion. Both overcome demons. I meet my own with tears: fear of compromise, of succumbing to a mechanistic solution, yet at the same time, realizing I wouldn't be here to choose if it hadn't been for those shock paddles. Trauma and rage are tucked away. I am still so tenuous in being alive.

As I lie awake at night, I begin to design a healing mandala, not out of invention, but from intuition—trusting the images that come. My lopsided heart is in the middle, bound by a circle of dear friends, those who hold me in the light. This heart is enclosed by the circle of ancestors, those on the other side who are close to me—my mother, my grandparents, my dear friend Ayesha, who just died two months ago of ovarian cancer. The next encircling is of angels. Then there are two crosses: Christ above, Sophia below, Raphael to the left, Michael to the right. If this were a compass, then in the northeast is Isis, balanced by Mary in the southwest. Tara is in the northwest position, across from Medicine Buddha in the southeast.

My mandala begins with a crude sketch that I keep refining. I delight in finding a color and prayer for each of these allies. I visualize this circle more and more clearly, until it becomes spatial as well as visual—a sounding and surrounding, a circling of strength to rely upon. I define the healing power of each being and use it in a prayer I compose as surgery approaches:

> *Radiant healing love of Christ,*
> *Sacred healing immanence of Sophia,*
> *Pure healing protection of Tara,*
> *Supreme healing awareness of Medicine Buddha,*
> *Deep healing mystery of Isis,*
> *Ever-enfolding healing grace of Mary,*
> *Divine healing breath of Raphael,*
> *And radical healing courage of Michael.*

Over the next few months, I will summon this mandala inwardly to ward off the insidious fear that creeps along beside me. I will rely upon the encircling of my ancestors, as I learn of terror and grace.

~⁊☙

*Early 1900s, 1960s*

## Enduring Lace

William and Mary-Cushing Howard, my maternal great-grandparents, died long before I was born, but snatches of their story
remain. As his nickname "Doc" suggests, my great-grandfather
was indeed a doctor, one in a line preceding him. Recently, I read
through my grandmother's album of old letters in sepia script
from his ancestors. One referred to grave-robbing committed in
order to obtain the cadavers necessary for an early 1800's medical
training—standard practice from the sound of it. I am disturbed
by the act of stealing the dead to promote a medical science that in
itself relies on an anatomy based on the components of a corpse.
Born in 1867, Doc was only a generation removed from these
off-base origins. In addition to being a physician, he did research
as a professor of pathology who "helped bring medicine into the
20th century," according to the university where he taught. He
was known for having developed something new in the practice
of percussion and auscultation—tapping and listening to how the
sound reverberates, to ascertain lung capacity, and determine the
size and placement of the living heart.

I picture him with the sharp features I've seen in his portrait, mustached with wire-rim spectacles and serious intent. Bent
over a patient, he taps out this percussion, curved fingers moving
slowly across the ribs, his gaze softening as he listens through his
stethoscope. Honed in refinement, he has done this thousands of
times. I picture him, his glance intensifying as he avidly discusses
his findings with fellow doctors: introducing his methodology,

presenting his findings, lecturing students on this practice still used in routine medical exams today, but of late devolving due to dependence on technology.

While Doc was engaged in this way, Mary-Cushing's fingers were occupied with a different precision: the making of fine crochet. I have a linen runner edged with delicate lace borders that she made. Her well-worn *Book of Common Prayer* dated from 1869, with its daily stitchings of blessings and praise, begins with instructions, "The *Psalter* shall be read through once every month, as it is there appointed, both for morning and evening prayer." Its bordered pages include sections of prayers such as "The Thanksgiving of Women after Childbirth," commonly called the "Churching of Women" and "The Order for the Visitation of the Sick" as well as "Forms of Prayer to be used at Sea." I wonder how many sea voyages she may have taken in her lifetime.

On my childhood visits to their turn-of-the-century home in Rhode Island, where my great-uncle Bill lived, I loved to venture away from the main house and follow the winding path through the woods to come upon the little one-room cabin that had belonged to her. Each time: a rediscovery. Perched on a bluff overlooking a cove of the river, her shingled green hut was used for storage, neglected and locked up by the time I knew it. I would stand on the weathered wooden porch and look in the windows. Through the cobwebs I tried to conjure up how it was back in her day.

For me, this cabin was capable of housing mermaids, wizards, and wise-women hermits who knew plant lore and healed animals. These images merged with one of my great-grandmothers in contemplative silence, her hands resting in rare stillness.

Mary-Cushing Howard's daughter, my grandma, took it as her entrusted duty to inform me of the matriarchal line of Mary-Cushings that we share, she the fifth and I the seventh. I always knew when her ancestral reveries were coming on by the way the gleam in her eye lasered in intensity. Almost sternly she would take me aside and begin, her voice deliberate and slow, "The first Mary-Cushing lived in revolutionary times. She was married to a doctor who served five counties in Massachusetts. In those days, the only mode of transport was horseback and he would take off for days at a time, whenever duty required. Why, he was even called out on their wedding night! That was how she started married life: she didn't see much of him! But no matter, she was a strong and independent woman, as all the Mary-Cushings were and are ... " and she'd fix me with her eye, an implied commandment in those words. As a child, I braced myself to tolerate the repetition of stories that I only gradually grew to cherish. She would ramble on through the generations, and always end with some variation of, "Now I know you never got to meet my mother. She adored music and was a devoutly spiritual person. She read all of Mary Baker Eddy and subscribed to her philosophy, in private." I imagine my great-grandmother in the solitude of her little cabin, wind rustling in the trees all around, following a way—based on faith in spiritual healing to the point of regarding all illness as illusion—in direct antithesis to her husband's profession.

This morning I consider this obvious opposition: an agnostic medical researcher and a woman drawn to healing of the spirit. Was this a tension between them? I won't ever know how it was expressed: spacious with respect or fraught with criticism. Did the privacy of her convictions include him? Was she impressed by his latest findings? I ponder what tensions were aired—or not—over the surviving linen that adorns my sideboard.

In me there lives a pragmatic man trained in observation. He taps his skilled fingers and listens closely in order to gauge the dimensions of the heart. *Tap tap tap.* He listens again, sounding the topography. In me there is, as well, a devoted woman. She folds her hands in prayer, and sings, praising the unity of all creation. These two share the same bed, household, family. A duality exists between them—his side, her side; contention and struggle as they bump up against each other. But there are moments of deep bow and embrace, the beginnings of a choreography of balance. I honor them both.

❧

*1958 – 1960s*

## Correspondences

I never had a name for her, my father's mother, although I have been told: Caro Elizabeth, Bess, Betty; that her maiden name was Prescott—her initials EPS. What I heard growing up was "Mother" in my father's serious tone, echoing vacancy. I had always been told that she had kept herself alive to meet me. She died shortly thereafter. As soon after my birth as we could travel, my parents took me from Philadelphia to Boston in order to see her, weak from stroke and in her eighties. Her last days, my first; she held me in warm welcome. That meeting, informed by love, is inscribed into me. Throughout my life I have recognized her presence, and don't limit knowing her to that one meeting in the flesh.

My father didn't tell us stories of his childhood yet, as he would later on in his life, but he gave information about his mother: she was a Swedenborgian and homeopath. It took awhile just to pronounce those names, let alone know what they meant. I sought her out in relics left behind: the wooden jewelry box that was passed on to my mother with some of her rings—sapphire, pearl, cameo; the tortoise shell hair combs that perplexed me as to how they would hold up hair; the glass and silver flask that must have held powder once, but was empty now, and tarnished. My father's father had died of Hodgkin's disease when my dad was six and his sister, four. Neither of them remembered their father at all, but his death left a void, unavoidable to note. It was almost forbidden by their mother to speak of him. After his death, they were left in various homes while their newly widowed mother earned money by serving as a traveling companion, until she remarried a few years later.

As a child, I would venture into my father's study to explore. On the top of stacks of boxes of old papers, there was an open shoebox full of copies of little booklets that his mother had written, printed by her second husband, a typographer who owned a press. Before I could read, I was compelled by those yellow covered books with the engraving of a mountain scene. Her words, his typeset imprinted upon fine laid paper, its lined pattern watermarked behind the words. When I could make out the title and discovered it was about death, I knew with a child's logic that, having died herself, my grandmother knew of these realms.

Later, when I was twelve or so, Dad gave me a copy of this pamphlet for my own. I kept it on my bureau at first, and then beside my altar when I created a shrine room to meditate in. I read through the pages many times of how death is so often misunderstood, of the body being shed to be born into another world, of heavenly beings, of Divine Providence (in capitals!) and the spiritual eye and ear. What intrigued me most was the explanation about the illustration on the cover—a pathway flanked by cypress trees beside a lake, leading to a mountain. "Swedenborg has given us wonderful material to use in illustrating what we write of this world and the next." She introduced "correspondences"—an understanding of the natural world as an expression of spiritual truths, which became a template of how I perceived the world.

When I was fourteen or fifteen, my curiosity about my grandmother grew and my father dug out an old leather binder of his mother's typed articles for me. These essays were printed in women's magazines, local papers and journals. She wrote regularly for a lay homeopathic journal and told of her great-great-grandfather, Dr. White from Maine, one of the first practicing homeopaths in the New World. She introduced remedies for lay people—the miracles of arnica and calendula, the many uses of *nux vomica* or *arsenicum album* and more, and how to maintain good magnetism in a sick room. She championed the home as a place of refuge from the harshness of the world, and a place to cultivate beauty, and opposed women painting their faces.

I often imagine what blessing she gave me as I lay, newborn in her arms. I picture her transmitting her wisdom, her mantle of protection, her promise to watch over me, as indeed, she has. The words are lost, but the imprint remains, impressed invisibly and carried on.

*1960s – early 1970s*

## Dream Temple

Grandfa's fingers were long. Besides that, I can't remember what my mother's father's hands looked like. Elegant? Strong? It is his touch that remains distinct, decades after his passing—a subtle emanation, radiant and soothing. Later, I would name it: healing energy. His essence: sapphire incandescence. In any spare moment of family gatherings, he'd give Grandma a massage as she lay on the couch, resting, and then offer a foot-rub to whomever might want one. I was always eager for his touch, infused, it seemed, with sky-high mountains.

Perhaps it was his love of the Himalayas that sounded through his hands. My grandparents had spent much time in India, beginning with living in Delhi when Grandfa worked to support the emerging government after independence. He was named Harry, "Hari" to the family, an endearment from Raihana, my grandparents' Sufi teacher in India. I heard many stories about Raihana as I grew up: how she was close to Ghandiji, how she was Muslim, but loved Krishna, the Hindu god whose picture was over my grandma's desk. I adored this crowned and garlanded being with long curly hair and a loving gaze; a golden flute poised to play. I insisted that Krishna had to be a woman, but Grandma only laughed and told me not all men looked or acted the way I was taught they should. She told me she had married a gentle man. That I could agree with.

When I was growing up, Hari would take time to give attention that was rare for me to receive from adults. I never saw him rushed. He sat with me and asked questions, always fascinated with what I was studying in school, from Greek myths to Leonardo to astronomy. With his blue eyes sparkling, he told me stories: the adventures of Brer Rabbit, or about his travels in distant lands or the behavior of elephants or making salad at Rev. Martin Luther King, Jr.'s home in Atlanta where he was once a guest.

During one visit to their home in Baltimore, when I was twelve or so, he invited me into his "shrine" room, which had always been off limits to the rest of us. Grandma, who openly talked to me about Raihana and past lives, made a big deal about this special privilege bestowed upon me. I had known that Hari got up at four every morning to meditate and this was where he went when the rest of the family was asleep. The petite room with its tiny window was startlingly still, vibrant with echoes of thousands of Oms intoned. There was a Muslim prayer rug to sit on and an altar with Hindu and Buddhist artifacts—a peacock fan, an ivory statue of Gandhi.

When I was in seventh grade, Hari noticed that I was seriously into dreams. It was easy to confide in him that I remembered six to seven dreams a night and wrote in a special journal to keep track of them. I was amazed by their vividness and light, although previously I had grueling nightmares. The summer I turned thirteen, in his slow and steady voice, he told me about Epidaurus, in ancient Greece, in the same matter-of-fact way he had told me about the habits of bears or how to forage for edible greens. "People came from all over Greece to sleep in a special hall—called the *enkoimitiria*. This was in the temple for Asklepius, the god of medicine. When they slept there, people were given dreams that revealed their cure. Sometimes it was obvious, but other times, the priests had to interpret what was in the dream. It was different for everyone."

He told me tales of Asklepius, raised by the centaur, Chiron. Athena gave him the blood from the severed head of the gorgon, Medusa: one vial from the left vein, and one from the right. One blood to cure, to restore life; and another—poison, to slay. I imagined the ancient temple where this first physician was honored—the stone enclosure, the sanctuary where cots were laid, surrounded by Doric columns, how the hush of sleep would fall upon those seeking healing after they offered themselves up to dreams. How in the morning, drowsy with sleep, each patient would tell of their dream and the priests would know how to treat them from what their dreams revealed.

I longed for that time when priest-physicians trusted in dream wisdom. I wanted to claim images that arose in my dreams as messages from spiritual beings. To know that each individual had their own particular way of healing offered a contrast to the jingles from Alka-Selzer and aspirin that blared from our TV set. Epidaurus provided a reference point—to which I could return. To know that dreams could reveal cure gave me sanctuary, enshrined within.

⸙

*1960s*
*Philadelphia*

## Walk-through

At six years old, I find my way through the human heart, accompanied by the loud *ta-dum, ta-dum* of the pulsating walls. We are at the Franklin Institute in downtown Philadelphia, visiting a walk-through model—"The Engine of Life," my favorite exhibit here. I step through the plastered chambers lit in blue at first, then shifting into red and dimming into shadow, as the thumping grows louder. *Ta-dum, ta-dum.* I move slowly at first to get accustomed to the darkness, then more rapidly as I get used to being within this unknown giant's heart. The way winds through dulled plaster surfaces shuddering in the constant rhythm. *Ta-dum, ta-dum.* I hold my breath as the path curves into a dank enclosure. Hands slightly clenched, I keep going, relieved when I emerge into the light at the end of the tunnel of aorta.

Then I run right round to the beginning again, drawn back in, as always. It stinks of old sneakers, grubby gray rubber stretched across the pathway mimicking membranes and simulating heart valves. *Ta-dum, ta-dum.* The paint has none of the luster or luminosity that I innately expect for the heart.

Decades later, I carry impressions from that shrine of anatomical correctness imprinted upon me: heart's anatomy from the inside. I chose as a child to go continuously through, over and over again, enacting the perpetual motion of circulation. When I become a heart patient, this first impression of a clumsy rendering of heart will echo as I struggle against the giant of the orthodox medical view. I will be subjected to all manner of measuring, from ECGs and Holter monitors to echocardiograms and stress tests: each providing a view of the heart. The model I become familiar with will no longer be of dull plaster, but presented on a flat screen: sound waves bombarding the heart invisibly to render back its form in cross sections. *Ta-dum, ta-dum.* I will hear its beat broadcast electronically as I watch blood flow volumes portrayed in glaring reds and blues. Systole, diastole. I will learn new names. I will see variations on those same chambers and valves that I knew in my childhood venture through shadow—atrium, tricuspid valve, ventricle, mitral valve, septum. Impaired. My heart, my children's hearts: cardiac specimens.

I will find a new terror, without the thrill I knew as a child, as I enter more deeply into each chamber. I will move cautiously at first, and then proceed. Inexplicably, I will hold out for luminosity. I will find many variations of heart structure and function within the range of "normal," and a fluidity of symptoms within any given defect. I will refuse to perceive my heart reduced to a malfunctioning machine. I will resist, yet eventually embrace a mechanistic view of the heart. I will claim a broader reference. I will find new images of heart, and eventually pass through.

⁓∾⊘

*Summer, 1975*
*Nevada City, California*

## Murmuring

High summer in the low Sierras. Day by blazing day, we dig clay, and fashion it into form. By night, I learn another heat—the geography of Brian's body. I become fluent in the touch that flows between us, but there is more to know. Darkness holds us as we nestle together, my ear pressed against his chest. Beneath the arcing vault of his ribs, an ocean sounds: waves pounding unevenly.

"Do you hear it?" he asks dreamily.

"Hm?" I ask.

"My heart murmur."

"The shushing?"

"Um-hum—there's a little hole between my heart chambers."

I think of the Japanese climbing kiln that we've been working with—the openings that allow the fire-path to ascend through the chambers.

Voice resonant in his chest, he continues, "It's a heart defect. I was born that way. So the blood flows through the hole and makes that extra *sssssh* at the end."

I keep listening to his heart's improvisation: a steady beat doubling in echo and whoosh reverberating. I will listen again and again, dreaming into this subterranean generosity. In the future, when I enter the arena of cardiac deviations, I will remember that intimacy—Brian's rhythm that I knew by heart.

*Mid 1970s – Mid 1990s*
*Upstate New York and Pacific Northwest*

## Woman of the Trees

My amulet is a tree woman, a woman-tree. Bud swell, blossom burst, leaves unfolding; she is all the trees whose bloom I have witnessed. Broadleaf, conifer; she is every tree I have cherished. Red leaf, seedpod: she is all women who honor their bond with the green growing world. Crown and anchor; she is all the trees that have offered refuge. Cork and cambium; she is each tree I have touched, hand palmed on naked trunk open to pulsation. Sap rising, sap falling; she is the channeling of living fire that streams through. Sunlight ingested, life force pervading; she is abundance of fruit offered forth. Sway and rustle; she is cry of forest endangered. Sapwood, core; she is women everywhere informed by that call, women of the trees.

> I know the weight of this pendent against my breast,
> the gravity of Artemis:
> Lady of Birch, of Fir, of Hazel;
> Lady of Beech, of Cedar, of Oak;
> Lady of Maple, of Cherry, of Willow

Through her I can trace my own dendrology as a woman of the trees, years marked in rings around the sapwood core. From refuge of low-lying hemlock boughs and majesty of maple in my childhood garden, to the cherry tree that grows into my room through my open window to blossom over my bed at fifteen, I am never far from green unfurling. Rings extend: from forest homes to urban dwellings, always close to the standing ones.

Close to the core here, a dendril ring thickens: In becoming a parent, I awaken to the future that lives in my children. How to insure a healthy biosphere for generations to come? A sense of urgency takes hold of me. As young mothers, a friend and I create one of many Universal Children's Gardens, affiliated with the United Nations and dedicated to world peace. Extending out from that, many rings will follow: tree-planting celebrations, forest and wetlands restoration projects with local children to support tree-planting efforts of children in Natal, South Africa. Global awareness: planetary links forged by Children of the Green Earth (CGE) founded on the vision of "The Earth made green again through the efforts of children planting trees."

When my daughter, Rose, is two, I take over running this international organization part-time. Outwardly, there is office work: answering inquiries, sending out resources, fundraising, banking and networking with other ecological organizations. Inwardly, there is a sense of fulfilling the inspiration of Richard St. Barbe Baker, founder of CGE. Known as "The Man of the Trees," he was a forester, responsible for the planting millions of trees in his lifetime. He started CGE in his nineties, traveling worldwide to raise awareness and establish tree-planting partnerships.

With so many references to The Man of the Trees around me, a natural counterpart becomes that of a Woman of the Trees. As wild-protectoress, she inspires this diligent work. Her heart is drenched in wild green. Guardian and guide, gracious in forest giving, riven through with green green green. She is Artemis in distress over clear-cuts, over the rapid diminishment of wetlands, insistent upon restorative will. I have a plaster cast of my face that I paint green. I gather offerings of the forest and decorate this green mask with birch and fir bark for skin, acorns for eyes and pine cone petals for brows, cherry blossoms for mouth and cedar branches for hair. She wears an alder-pod crown.

Woman and tree interfuse. A slash to one becomes a gash in another. This way akin to what has been instilled in me by Artemis—a myriad of creatures interwoven, one breath; a multitude of beings intertwined, one body. One wild heart unites us.

～❧～

*Summer, 1993*
*Whidbey Island, Washington*

## Wounding Vision

The more deeply I have devoted myself to raising my children as a spiritual practice, the further I have drifted from the transcendent forms of Sufi meditation that I've practiced for years. I am leading a Deep Ecology ritual in The Marsh House, an octagonal hall with wide windows on six sides overlooking a meadow. The path that leads here winds through a marsh, bordered with the heart-shaped deep green foliage of wild ginger. We've walked here through the rustle of alder, the silver-gray-barked tree that bleeds flame brilliant when cut, a radiance hidden behind demure tones.

Wrapped in a green shawl, I sit facing forty people or so, many from the Sufi community. Light streams in. I invoke the presence of the spirit of Gaia, our planet home, flesh of our flesh. I encourage awakening to indigenous self, to reclaim the wisdom encoded within, weaving spirit in to instinct. I speak of expanding our sense of identity to include our bond to the myriad forms of life that are at peril, of the raw grief that this loss holds.

I say, "To prepare for the Cairn of Mourning, go outside and find a place to sit in contemplation. Find one particular aspect of nature's suffering that strikes you and bring back a stone to stand for that. When we return, we will create a cairn, a pile of stones, as we name these losses." I stand. "I'll beat a drum for about twenty minutes. When you hear it again at a different tempo, it will mean it is time to come back in. Please remain silent." The group disperses. People walk off with blankets and pillows, across the meadow, into the forest, out onto the marshland paths.

I stay close to the meadow, right by the great Douglas fir whom I call "Grandmother." She towers above, surely guardian of this place, sovereign among Northwest trees. Her creased trunk is layered, inlaid with bark molded in rivering wrinkles, the ground soft with her rusty needles, an occasional cone scattered. Sharply pungent, she emanates through the meadow, starry branches cascading from her wide girth. She sways and waves in the slight breezes. The sun illuminates the meadow by the marshlands, frogs silent in the golden streaming day.

I stand with my frame drum—deer skin stretched over a wide hoop of yellow cedar. Holding it by the soft suede wrapped around the cross of sinews, I brush my fingers across the dry uneven grain. Taut. I stand with my feet bare in the soft give of fir needles. Toes spread, I press slightly down, sole to soil. A subtle rooting extends from me down into the Earth. Breath deepening, I take up the padded manzanita beater and begin to strike the drum:

*DUM! DUM! DUM! DE DUM!*
*... deep tones vibrating ...*
*DUM! DUM! DE DUM!*

Inwardly, I summon the ancestors. I open to the spirit-guardians of the land, those whose lives have become the ground we stand upon, roots and foundation. A current rises up and through me, a circulation I honor. Pulsation. Heart beat. Drumming. I am carried inwardly to a sacred grove, this image always my doorway to deeper perception. A greater breath streams through.

Dissolve into the current of drumming—dreaming, Earth's thrum enters me.

Brim. Rumble. Crumble. Crash.

*I am wrenched into clear-cut ... a vast stretch of ground gashed from trees uprooted, scattered stumps left jagged. I ache for the fallen grove and know that the felling continues.*

*Struck, I extend to riverbeds choked with debris of shredded forests, waters fouled and spoiled. No wetlands. Not a bird sings. I ache for the memory of green.*

*Parched, I extend into a shroud of toxic haze, shocked by grid and gray of existence sheared from source. I ache for memory of ebb and flow ever-circling.*

*Leaden, I extend into an enormity of angular oppressions. Obliteration in asphalt: crisscross of roads, cinderblock and blockade. No curve, no horizon. I ache for spacious bend beyond constriction.*

*Narrowed, I extend to glimpse generations to come. In the shell of cities, shadow people drift listless, dulled and deprived. Stunted children gasp for breath. My bloodline, children of my children, starkly dimmed and doomed. I ache for memory of wild embrace.*

Trance receding, I slow the drumming, then clamp the final beat, stick against drum. Done. But there is a pounding in my chest that doesn't stop, fast and dashing. I open my eyes gradually, dazed a bit by the dazzle of sun, the sudden green. I have dreamt

of wastelands before, and this one will haunt me. The fir branches
rustle behind me. No harm visible. I stand on the edge of the welcome meadow, in perfect calmness. Except for my heart. Literally.

*Quick, quick, my heart, so quick ... quick, quick, my heart ...*

Never mind. I walk, drumming again in a measured rhythm,
to summon the group back to our meeting place so the ritual can
begin. We gather in two loose circles, one within another. I kneel
in the inner circle, still drumming.

After opening with a ceremonial song, I invoke the Ancestors aloud now, the Grandmothers with their chord of ancient and
sustained care. With a poem, I invite Artemis into our presence,
not as static figure, but as a living presence to counter extinction
of all those beings that we love. I call on her as moon maiden with
a rainbow quiver; I invoke her as wild protectoress, she of the
streaming green whose domain is the untamed places, guardian of
forest creatures, intimate with mountains and wild woods.

Only later will I remember that she is also stalking huntress,
that in her mythic dimension, it is her arrows that bring illness
as well as healing to women. Artemis: free and fierce and caring,
bow flexed and ready, dark arrows/light arrows, aimed at the heart
of woman. I will wonder if, in that moment, my apppeal to her
caused her bow to be loosed. I became target to an invisible arrow.
Was I her quarry?

*Quick, quick, my heart, so quick ... quick, quick, my heart ...*

I hardly notice these palpitations. Instead, as if conjuring, I
implore the suffering of the living Earth to be present, felt strongly
enough to inspire a difference. With a heart-shaped iron bell the

size of my palm, I invoke animals, endangered or extinct, from Joanna's Bestiary,[1] beginning,

> *Short-tailed albatross*
> *Whooping crane*
> *Gray wolf*
> *Peregrine falcon*
> *Hawksbill turtle*
> *Jaguar*
> *Rhinocerous*
> *Reed warbler*
> *Swallow tailed butterfly*
> *Manx shearwater*
> *Indian Python*
> *Howler monkey*
> *Blue whale ...*

I continue on, clunking iron with iron for each name—the thud of grave finality. But my heart is not a-thud, rather it is quivering wildly, an undercurrent as I give instructions. "One by one, we will each bring a stone up to create a cairn to stand for all that we mourn for the living planet. As you place your stone, please say aloud what it represents." One stone for each sorrow, a marking of our regrets.

I take a round gray stone from my pocket and go to the center of the room, stooping down. "I place this stone to honor the future generations who will suffer because of our inability to take them into account." I rest the stone on the empty floor. I step back and sit, taking my place in the circle.

One by one, others follow.

"This is for the oceans that have become dumping grounds."

" ... the diminishing butterflies."

" ... the loss of the bluebird."

" ... the air that is no longer pure."

" ... the eastern forests that are sickly and dying because of acid rain."

" ... the groundwater that is being taken faster than it can be replenished."

"I mourn the loss of coral reefs."

Stone by solemn stone, the cairn has been erected. In a tone of dirge, the ritual ends. Somber. This is the first step in creating a sensitization, in a longer process that will continue over the weekend. The next day will bring a lighter tone, a celebration. But for now the heaviness of stones abides. In the stillness I feel another weight:

*Quick, quick, my heart, so quick ... quick, quick, my heart ...*

Still pounding. What is this racing in my body? This throbbing so taut, this knotting round my shoulder blades, this churn of heart?

I trust it will subside.

～✦

It is time for a break and I am wondering how my kids are doing, at the beach with their day camp. Rosy is three years old; tagging along with the brothers she adores: Kyrian, six; Emmanuel, nine; Chris, thirteen. I am wondering why my heart is beating as if I am extremely nervous, when I'm not. People stand and leave the room quietly, some stopping to thank me on the way out with a smile and bow or a hug. No one speaks.

After stretching, the group is back, kneeling close in a large circle. Saraswati, an old friend, composes herself and her bell-like voice as she introduces the session. "We will concentrate on our individual hearts being shattered in order to accommodate the divine." She gives instruction on the movements of the ancient incantation.

Intoning the sacred phrase, I let myself expand into vastness and then let it converge in a small point, arrow of breaking through my singularity. The whole tradition of mystic Sufi poetry glorifies this breaking the shell of the heart in order for the newborn soul to arise.

> *Heart ailing, heart breaking—*
> *this is the heart's terrain:*
> *in knowing love, we know pain.*
>
> *What could be more common?*
> *Yet each shattered heart is so singular,*
> *each one probes the divine.*
> —Variation on Rumi

Echoing ocean in rise and fall, the swell and crash of waves breaking. My heart an exaggerated echo of continuous boom. Counterpoint to the soothing murmur in the room, an acceleration has taken hold of me. The onset of my heart's labor has begun.

❧

*July, 1993*
*Seattle*

## Cardiac Consultation III: Broken Chord

We're home again after being up on Whidbey Island. Once the kids settle in, and I get the first load of laundry going, I call my naturopath. I want to ask him what a normal pulse is, not from conscious alarm as much as curiosity. When he hears my heart rate has been at 130 beats per minute with cramping and shortness of breath for two days and one sleepless night, his usual mellow manner evaporates and he sends me immediately to the E.R. I am stunned at the incongruence that he, so conservative in his use of standard medical practices, would recommend a hospital. It begins to dawn on me that something might actually be wrong here.

Wrong enough to leave Rosy with her brothers for the first time, which luckily she is excited about as we slip out the door. With my husband Atum bewildered beside me, I enter alien ground. I am eventually passed from the emergency room to Zenith Cardiology, across the hospital campus. We meet with Dr. D, a mild-mannered graying forty-something man of medium stature. As he moves a cold stethoscope above and below my left breast, I watch his eyes, behind wire rim glasses, grow intent: first with concentration, then with recognition. After listening, he unfastens the stethoscope from his ears, steps back, stands tall and says, "Well, you have quite a significant heart murmur here. Chances are that you have had a mitral valve prolapse already. It's a fairly common condition." He shows us a diagram, pointing out the valve on the left side of the heart and the tendrils that held it in place. "Probably in the last few days, a chord in the valve broke so that it won't close properly." I try to picture this rift as I learn an anatomy new to me, brought to attention by a persistent drumming of late.

"The good news is that this kind of deterioration is corrected quite successfully with valve replacement surgery, but you will need to take care of this in the next few days."

When I ask what would happen if I don't have the surgery, his eyes furrow, he looks at me sharply and pronounces, "If you don't replace your damaged valve right away, it will continue to deteriorate and you will become weaker and weaker. If you don't take care of it soon, you won't live to see your children grow up." In that sterile room, I enter the journey that will take me to cardiac experts and to various healers, through shifts in diagnosis and hubris, through wounding and grace, full circle to Humble, Texas.

I am put on medication and sent home to bed, having been told that the operation should be scheduled in two days time, after a test to confirm the diagnosis. In two days it will also be my 35th birthday. No one, least of all me, can believe it. How can this be?

The next day, my dear friend Patti brings me a bracelet with beads from each member of our woman's circle, imbued with their blessings and best wishes. It won't be long until another bracelet will grace my wrist beside it: Medic Alert. Patti, whose husband is a doctor, is familiar with surgery. She gently but firmly tells me what to expect.

"I want you to be prepared for this because it's a big deal. First they saw through your ribs and open them ... "

This radical break and entry goes against all that I believe in when it comes to healthcare. I am a seventh generation homeopath, raised under the care of one of the few homeopathic doctors left in the 1960s, before this form of medicine was gradually revived in the United States. A "holistic" approach was something that I have taken for granted, even before that term was in usage. I gave birth naturally, at home, to all four of my children and I champion the cause of non-intervention. Indeed, I have always looked upon the hospital as the last resort, a failure. Trained as a layperson in homeopathy and attending a score of homebirths as a midwife's assistant, I have more than once successfully dispensed remedies for uterine inertia rather than resorting to the backup of the hospital for Pitocin to induce labor. I have always considered antibiotics aberrant, having never taken an aspirin, and have been called "rugged" by the dentist because I refuse to take Novocain. I intercepted surgery for my husband's appendicitis attack with homeopathy and used cranial osteopathy (with the originators of this treatment, old family friends in their nineties at the time) to open my newborn son's overlapping fontanel rather than the standard skull surgery. I have always relied upon and trusted natural healing, which has served my family and me just fine.

Until now.

But, explore as I might, there doesn't seem to be any alternative, no remedy to stitch up a floppy heart valve. I resign myself as best I can.

Later that day, in preparation for impending surgery, Atum and I return to the hospital for an echocardiogram, a sonic charting of my heart. After introducing himself, a young man, Dan, leads me back to a small room dominated by a screen and keyboard, with a place to lie down beside it. At my request, he positions the screen so that I can peek into the mystery revealed there. I gaze at a dynamic mandala, four chambers pulsating, various angles of the whooshing flower of heart. For the first time, I witness the astonishing beauty of that fluid organ at work in beat and flow. I am introduced to ventricle, septum, aorta, valves. I watch as the technician's face grows puzzled.

When the test is over, Dr. D, clearly flustered, takes Atum and me into his windowless office. Slowly, he tells us that the echocardiogram has revealed a rare heart condition, far more severe than a valve problem. With dismay, he tells us this can't be fixed as easily with surgery. Using a model, painted plastic creaking open on a hinge, he shows us the septum, the core muscle of the heart, dividing the left chamber from the right. In my case, he says, the septum is enlarged so that it presses against the mitral valve, keeping it open when it should close completely during the heart's contraction.

As for surgery, he explains that it would consist of cutting out some of that muscle, and it is risky. I decline. Nervous but in command, he tells us of the mechanics of this heart disease, of the risks involved in having it. Prominent among them is what is clinically referred to as "excess sudden deaths." In a patient handout this is addressed as "the most unpredictable and devastating complication." It's the same condition that athletes drop dead in action from, with no warning.

He tells me to prepare myself for this possibility, but to also understand that it isn't always the case. This is a chronic condition to live with under its limitations: medication, rest, no physical exertion. It is possible, he tells us, that I could live, under care, for another twenty years or more. It is also possible that if I strain my heart, I could overtax it, leading to the "devastating complication."

In that sterile room, another sentence was also being given. I would only see it years later, from the other side of my dissolved marriage. Much of the distance that would come between Atum and me originated in the revelation of that moment. My threatened mortality would begin disintegrating what had been a long and fruitful union. The possibility of death did us part.

On a drug company's complimentary pad of paper beside a colored graphic cross-section of a heart, at my request, Dr. D writes out the name of my disease: Asymmetric Septal Hypertrophy with LVOT (Left Ventricle Outflow Track) Obstruction, Mitral Valve Prolapse with Severe Regurgitation. This condition is characterized by a thickening of the septal muscle in the left ventricle. This results from the actual structure of the cardiac cells being whorled rather than linear, similar to scar tissue (myocardial fiber disarray). This enlargement decreases the amount of blood that can flow into the left heart chamber. In a normally functioning heart, the valves open and close completely, expand and contract, regulating the blood flow rhythmically. But by remaining partially open (as in my case) the blood is not clearly ejected through the valve, but swishes around. This sloppy circulation is audible as a heart murmur, whoosh echoing the *da-dum / da-dum* of heart beat.

Here's what "mitral insufficiency" sounds like in Hurst's, the bible of cardiac texts: "These structures may be bent abnormally by the bulging ventricular septum with resulting excessive tension on the chordae tendineae preventing closure of the mitral orifice." These kinds of descriptions, although often requiring decoding, will become familiar to me. At the beginning, it is enough to simply master the name: obstructive hypertrophic cardiomyopathy, HCM for short, as it is often referred to (some add an O to designate when it is obstructive, thus becoming HOCM). There have been more different names for this particular disease than any other (seventy-five and counting), one bearing the subtitle "idiopathic," meaning, "we have no clue."

A few days later, Marianne, my health-care research-oriented midwife friend, brings photocopies of cardiac texts to me as others have brought bouquets. With a medical dictionary in hand, I examine these technical pages. My curiosity mixes with alarm as I identify with the detailed accounts of abnormalities. This is especially true when I come to the necropsy photos of cardiac structure accounting for sudden death. "Female, 36, died during an episode of rapid heart rate." Please, let that not be me.

❧

*Summer, 1993*
*Seattle*

## Lopressed

In a departure from my normally all-consuming life as a mother of four, I suddenly have to rest. A lot. The prescription I have been given (a beta-blocker) is a cardiac muscle relaxant, commonly used to lower blood pressure. The medication tames the rapid pulse rate of my overly contracting heart as it tries to compensate for the leaky valve. How many words are there for slow? Mix them together with what my prescription is actually called—Lopressor—and its name may begin to capture the influence of the drug. Low, pressed, and listless; lethargic and dragging, encumbered constantly, chronically weary. My already low diastolic/systolic has plummeted. The common adage to "slow down" becomes literal. Maneuvering my dulled drugged body is an effort. Climbing a flight of stairs tires me to the point of having to stop, every eight steps or so, to catch my labored breath. This is not an occasional episode. It is constant. How many times a day does a mother of four climb a flight of stairs?

The first danger of heart failure has passed and I am no longer limited to bed rest, yet every afternoon I lie down to combat the persistent weariness that besieges me. By afternoon, any stamina is drained away completely. I nap when possible or otherwise participate in whatever way I can, supine on the king-size bed with Kyrian and Rosy, my younger ones, around me. I read a lot of books aloud, tell stories, build with blocks on the rumple of covers, play puppets, enacting various characters from pirates' captive to grandmother. In recompense for being still, I take up beadwork. Kyrian readily joins me, delighted to string together bright glass. With beads of silver and amber, the crystallized resin of trees, I remake my medic-alert bracelet, my identity as invalid linked with the healing properties of ancient trees.

I am used to being strong and handling a lot on my own since Atum constantly travels for his work, often for weeks at a time. For the first time, I accept help. No lifting groceries, laundry, children: doctor's orders. This diminishment is a shock to all the family. Marcia, a generous artist whom I just met on Whidbey Island (at the Council of All Beings weekend, where the Cairn of Mourning was performed), comes regularly to help out—cleaning the house and playing with the children while I rest.

A doctor friend, Morris, after having talked with the cardiologist, and doing his own research, interprets my condition for me. He shares his grim conclusion over dinner, recommending a one story house so I won't have to deal with stairs. He makes an effort to be cheerful, pointing out that, "You may find one of the sole pleasures that you have left in life is to eat, so enjoy it." He sounds so upbeat. But I am not hungry. He meets with the boys to inform them about my state; not to expect much of me, to help out as best they can. Kyrian begins to make his own toast, slathering it with butter and honey and a generous shake of cinnamon.

Usually frugal and preferring thrift stores to new merchandise, I splurge on new bedding —"Italian Garden," a set of fine cotton sheets of larkspur and lily, dappled with purples and azure. I figure I am spending so much time in bed, I deserve it. It requires an effort to get over the feeling that it is my death bed. But those sheets will fade and wear out over time. I will eventually use them as rags.

*August, 1993*
*Bethesda, Maryland*

## Cardiac Consultation IV:
## The Disease with Seventy-Five Names

On a scorching July morning, with Atum accompanying me in a tender daze, we arrive by subway to the campus of the National Institute of Health (NIH) outside of Washington, D.C. My cardiologist encouraged me to seek the top researchers in hypertrophic cardiomyopathy and now I am visiting this place, the size of a small town, for the first time. It turns out that Suria, a dear friend of ours, has a brother, Michael, who is working at NIH as a medical photographer.

We find the Patient Services building and the cafeteria where I've arranged to meet Michael: Breakfast scents waft in the air. The room clamors with people in white coats and, just as we pause to survey the scene, a slight man in with dark curly hair steps toward us, his shining eyes inquisitive, "Mary?"

"Michael!" I could have spotted him anywhere, the resemblance to his sister, uncanny. With warm brown eyes and lean faces, they both bear the striking imprint of their German Jewish/

Cherokee heritage. We all laugh at the ease of recognition and shake hands, introducing ourselves. Over orange juice and coffee, Michael asks about my diagnosis and I tell him the specifics, still clumsy with the medical terms.

In the shocked gloom of being a heart patient, I'm soothed by Michael's animated warmth. He shows us to registration, then down the hall to get an ECG. A personal guide, he seems to know every other person, greeting them with cheery hello's and how y'doin's. After my ECG is done, Michael takes us up to the clinic, waits there with us until it's time for my echocardiogram. When my name is called, he walks beside me back to the lab, "I know all these guys, let me introduce you."

"Hey, Rudy," Michael says as he playfully slaps a dark, heavy-set middle-aged man on the back. "This is my friend Mary. You be good to her." Rudy hands me a gown as Michael turns on his heel and says, "I'll meet you back in the lobby when you're done."

Rudy's smile fades and, almost gruffly, he gets down to business, pulling the classic hospital green curtains around where I stand by the bed as he says, "Tell me when you're ready and we'll get on with it."

I take off my summer dress off and put the gown around me, loosely lacing the ties I know will be undone in moments. I slide the curtains open. As Rudy rips off the backing of the stick-on electrodes, I venture, "Would it possible for me to watch the echo?"

He shakes his head as he presses an electrode onto my chest, "Sorry, it's not set up that way." As I lie beside the monitor, accompanied by the amplification of my heart whoosh, I watch Rudy instead. Before I have time to ponder how his dull gaze contrasts with my own fascination, he mutters, "Okay, all done."

"Is that all?"

"Uh-huh."

I glance up at the clock, surprised by the brevity: five minutes. When I'm dressed and pull the curtain aside again, Rudy, who does this all day long, is all set with a new folded gown, ready for the next patient.

While we wait in the clinic, I look around at others who share my condition: an Indian family, the man in a turban and the woman in a sari; a young black woman who was on the subway; an elderly gentleman; a mother with her young son. In the quiet edginess of waiting, I regard these fellow patients as if my eyes could probe through layers of anatomy to see their malformed hearts, the thickened walls, the disrupted circulation.

Back in a small examination room I give my medical history, unremarkable until this summer, to a nurse. Then Dr. Fananapazir, the department head, sweeps in, looks over my records in a precursory way, shakes my hand and welcomes me. In the same breath, he offers me a pacemaker (their current research) and then whisks away, leaving us with his assistant, who trailed in behind him. A bright and efficient looking woman, Dr. L is a research doctor from Ireland. After she examines me, noting the gradient of my heart murmur, I turn on my tape recorder, take out my list of questions and begin to interview her.

She tells me my heart was fully grown by the time I was twenty and won't grow anymore, and agrees that it is mysterious that symptoms have manifested now. She goes on to discuss limitations, more liberal in her approach than what I have heard so far. As far as moving to a one story house, she recommends that we wait and see. I am told that my chest pain is from a mismatch between blood supply and the heart muscle.

Dr. L warns us that this is a genetic disease, that all of my kids could be at risk for developing it, that they will need to be checked out when they are full grown. She emphasizes that I am a good candidate for acquiring a pacemaker. Eagerly, she tells me how well my heart fits the protocol for their research. They're pioneering the use of pacemakers to alter the pattern of the contractions of the heart, to be timed to reduce the obstruction of the blood flow through the heart. After an animated description, she quiets down and confesses that there was no evidence that this or the drug therapies "alter how long you will live."

After a brief silence, I ask, "How, if I am on medication that sedates my heart like this, will I be able to tell if my heart symptoms ever change?"

Dr. L pauses a moment, sighs, apparently touched by this admission of innocence, and spells it out for me. "Well, it just wouldn't happen. It isn't possible for this condition or its symptoms to alter. Ever. There is certainly nothing in medical research to substantiate such a change. This is a condition that lasts a lifetime, and if your meds work or you get a pacemaker and you are lucky, it might be a long lifetime."

Silently, I refuse to believe my condition can't change. I see my heart as radiant in defiance against her claims.

*August, 1993*
*Bethesda, Maryland*

## Pickled Heart

Leaving Atum hidden behind the pages of *USA Today* in the waiting room, I follow Michael up another floor and down another hall in yet another building. He stops beside me to unlock the metal door to the laboratory where he works as a medical photographer.

"These labs are off limits to the public, but for you ... ," he says with a flourish. As he pushes the door open, I am overwhelmed by the reek of formaldehyde. It brings memories of the grade-school science room cluttered with stuffed dead animals, where I once fainted over dissection. Michael switches on glaring lights to reveal a stark, sterile room. No taxidermy here. "Welcome to my studio," he jokes. Shelves with plastic covered buckets line one concrete wall. A corner is filled with photography equipment and portable lights. A few cold steel tables stand in the center of the room. No windows. There is a steel sink with a high curved faucet, metal trays stacked beside it. Even on this summer day, the air here is chill. I shiver. Michael pulls up a stool beside a table, "Have a seat." Grateful to rest after the exertion of walking here, I wait.

"Now let's see ... " He surveys the buckets on the shelves. It takes me a minute to comprehend that we are surrounded by the coronary specimens he works with, as in cardiac, as in heart. As in: buckets of preserved human hearts all around us.

"Here," he says, as he carries over a container and places it on the table. It is labeled "Bryn Mawr." Not far from where I grew up. He opens the top and scoops out a heart from the liquid, letting it drip a moment. "Look. This is an example of HCM—your condition." He moves it closer to me. "This heart is probably a bit larger than yours."

I stare at the dead flesh in his hand, larger than my fist. It resembles models of the heart, yes, turnip-shaped in its taperings, but it is the color of liver in a butcher's case. I have never seen a preserved body part, only replicas, approximations. Fascinated and repelled, I stammer, "It looks so ... gray."

He laughs, "Yep. It's the pickling process." The heart lies sideways in his hand. Carefully, he lifts it apart where it has been sliced through with precision. I lean closer in to look more carefully at the chambers and valves. He points to the dividing muscle, "See, here is the septum with an abnormal thickening."

"Ahuh," I murmur.

"Do you want to hold it?"

"Sure," I say, unsure.

I reach out my cupped hands and he slides the lifeless organ into them. I've studied diagrams, but in this moment anatomical names fade away. A human heart lies in my hands. I am holding a heart that belonged to someone. Past tense. I shift it to rest on the palm of my left hand and slowly turn the brownish gray muscle around, to see all angles from the outside. Then, tremulously but determined, I open it to peer in. I behold the chambered formation: meat of muscle and lacework of leaflets. I scrutinize the shape of pathology my own heart shares with this anonymous specimen. It's the mitral valve that most astonishes me—the intricacy of its chordai, translucent strands so delicate, designed surely to billow in the sea. I notice how the enlarged septal muscle presses up towards the ventricle. Michael traces it with his finger. "See. When the heart is beating this would impinge on it, keeping it slightly open." He gives a little squeeze, forcing the valve open. "Like so."

Like mine. A heart gone wrong.

It takes an effort of imagination to translate this still object into a pulsating organ, kept busy with dual vortexes of blood. Over a hundred years ago, in a similar laboratory no doubt, an anatomist took a nameless heart like this (minus the defect) and boiled it for six hours and then soaked it in alcohol for two weeks. Only then was it soft enough to separate out the intricate layers of the myocardium: seven layers of muscle interlaced in a complex spiraling formation. All I see here is dense meat.

"Pretty neat, huh?" asks Michael. "I'm going to shoot it today." Seven layers undivided will be pinned open under a spotlight while Michael takes pictures. One angle and then another. He is one of many who pry open heart specimens, who probe coronary structures, who detail their deviations. Whoever's heart this was, with its bulging septum, it will become documented, part of the growing body of literature on this newly-discovered disease.

I hand the heart back to Michael. My hands feel oddly cold. He slides the preserved heart back into its bucket.

The splash ripples out into silence.

❧

*Autumn, 1993*
*Seattle*

## Night Race

It is night. Night when I should be sleeping but the darkness is not soft; it is harrowing. My heart is galloping against the silence, slamming at a wild pace. Will I make it till sunrise? The house is drenched in my children's dreaming.

How could I not be here to wake them in the morning?

Chris with his flashes of curiosity; Emmanuel with ponderous thoughts—too fast, too fast—not to tie Rose's sunbonnet around her chin. My heart is throbbing—not to tie Kyrian's shoes?—too fast, too fast—not to thread the beading needle for his little fingers—the knot of heart pain spreads down my arm—not to tie off balloons for their birthday parties to come—too fast, too fast—not to tie up all the loose ends.

My heart gallops against the silence. Not to drive carpool, overhearing conversations, not to answer random questions or ask "How was school?" My heart is hammering ... not to help out with homework or cozy up at story time, not to sing lullabies or whisper, "Sweet dreams."

This darkness clenches me in terror—not to make Sunday pancakes or daily school lunches—my heart is racing too fast, too fast. Not to watch my beloveds grow ...

My heart is thundering against the void—of no more laughter of no more song of no more words no more touch no more sweet scent of their sleep no more waking no more no more. No more. My heart is speeding towards a destination I did not choose.

❧

## Mother Goddess

Earth Mother. Goddess. Earth Mother Goddess. The clay pendant rests in my hand. The size of a thumbprint, she is a replica of one of the ancient figurines predating weapons or war. She is round, the droop of her breasts pronounced on her full belly. There is the slightest indication of hands, folded on the sides of her belly. She is rounded off with thunder-thighs, no legs below. From behind, her bum looks like an inverted heart. Her image is in rich currency among middle-aged women as we drift further from the culturally sanctioned norm of beauty. We look to her to remind ourselves there are other terms and once they were honored. Worshipped, even. She is also known as a goddess of love, Patti told me when she presented this figure as a gift to me. In addition, she is a fertility charm, which made us laugh, sagging mother of four that I am.

The goddess in my hand is the rounding down to womb and breast, embodied by me for many years. No head. No feet to go anywhere. For a long time, it was all I wanted for myself. Originally, this was my act of rebellion against a long line of suffragettes and feminists. In the nineteen-twenties, my grandmother was one of the first women to receive a master's degree in economics. My mother dedicated her life to low-income housing reform, lobbying in D.C. and founding a prominent housing organization. One aunt worked in the Secretariat at the United Nations; my other aunt was a key figure in draft resistance during the Vietnam war and became a lawyer for union workers. I reacted against the familial expectations to aggressively pursue a successful career. While my mother focused on affordable housing, I was left at home to be "cared for" by someone mentally unstable and abusive. As a result, I wanted to prove the value of embracing motherhood completely, compelled to fulfill that role and function.

Before I became a mother, I had graduated from high school with no intention of going to college and was busy becoming a dancer. Tentative and awkward at first, I gave myself to dance, again and again, pushing through the doubt and hesitancy, pushing through and continuing. It wasn't long until it was hours a day. Evening classes—weekly, bi-weekly, five nights a week. Intensives, a summer residency. My collection of leotards and footless tights grew, in varied hues until my whole wardrobe was that of a dancer's. Practice. Warming up and stripping down and sweating. Phrase of foot, arch of back and arc of arm. Contract and extend. Leap and land. Drill of repetition and thrill of the same movement sequence opening to effortlessness. The ecstasy and grind of it; surrender and grace.

Dancing entranced. The bold intimacy of meeting others through the vocabulary of movement. No plan to follow, improvisation relied on instinct. The vibrant sonic textures of the synthesizer borne out through body; bending in rise and fall; undulation and turn in accord with the fierce beat of the conga drums. Expressing resonance in rhythm and breath; in rhythm and current; in rhythm and resistance. The thrum of finding rhyme with another, seeping into dancing beyond a given choreography.

Years later, that sumptuous dance transformed into the dance of motherhood. I leapt into becoming a mother with delight, discovering each of my children in their distinctiveness—Chris, with his witty insight and articulation of the absurd; Emmanuel, whether eager or subdued, always adventurous and compassionate; Kyrian jumping with creative exuberance; Rose, mastering ornamentation from early on, imaginative and loving. In each pregnancy my heart grew full to overflowing, as spirit became flesh within me. Every time, I reveled in the primal creativity of a baby becoming through unfolding embryonic growth. There was urgency in me to devote myself completely to the service of another.

And another. And another. And another. I oriented myself entirely to motherhood: cradle of becoming and sustaining. Rounded in the softness of it, the breastfullness. I was at my best full melon-bellied, dreaming and feeding each child into being, tending angelic flame.

Heart and womb. Both are muscled organs overlaying openness; fibrous bands wrapping round hollow space. Heart and womb. Both share a capacity to contract, to contain. The muscles of the heart spiral round from its apex, a shape shared with galaxies. This whirling pulses in the subtle body as well: a wheel of energy parallel to the heart of flesh, a swirl in circulation. Rendered as a lotus, this heart's gestation seeded by love, empty of self, filled with another. A mother's heart: all embracing.

⤳

*August, 1993*
*Harlemville, New York*

## Cardiac Consultation V: Reading the Symptoms

Tara, my dear friend of over a decade, is driving me during my visit to The Abode, the Sufi community in the Berkshires, where we lived for six years. A stony silence creates an unusual space between us in her old brown Saab as the summer greens of farmlands and the Taconic hills flash by. Later she will tell me that she was paralyzed by the fear of losing me.

She's brought me to an appointment with an Anthroposophical doctor, Philip Incao. I met him when we lived at The Abode and he cared for the baby I delivered in a snowstorm when the midwife didn't make it. I had taken newborn Oliver and his mom to Dr. Incao for the exam where he informed her that Oliver had Down's syndrome. It turned out he had a severe heart defect, too. Here I was again, the heart patient now. In the flowing pastels of the lazured painted waiting room, Tara knits a mohair vest while Dr. Incao extends this last appointment of the day and ends up spending hours with me.

Anthroposophical medicine was developed by Rudolf Steiner as an aspect of the Spiritual Science that he founded. It incorporates a dynamic and far-reaching perception of health and illness based on the totality of the human being, and takes into account the invisible world. As a parent in a Waldorf school, I had been introduced to Steiner's work and recently completed a parenting course in this holistic approach to early childhood. That study opened me up to a deeper way of seeing, giving practical applications of the spirituality implicit in raising children. I trust that I can find wisdom in this non-mechanistic approach to medicine as well.

With a deeply caring manner, Dr. Incao takes time to be with me. He studies my test results, and asks about my history. Time slows down as he listens attentively. He sees a direct correlation between having been abused by my "caretaker" as an infant and what is manifesting for me physically now. He looks deeply into the "forces," as he calls them, behind my heart's deformity. All that he prescribes for me is aimed at contraction and closure to help offset my tendency to be overly open. He sees that my inability to seal off, as it were, has gone right down to the structure of my physical heart, with its floppy mitral valve.

I return home to Seattle with a stash of remedies and, following Dr. Incao's recommendations, begin to work with a curative Eurythmist, Glenda Monasch. This healing modality consists of movements that have an effect on a subtle level. In my case, they address the energetic imprint of trauma. In addition, I begin working with Ingrid Schiutevoerder, a practitioner of Process Oriented Psychology. This body-oriented approach evolved from Arnold Mindell's Jungian training, with a good dose of the shamanic thrown in. Instead of disavowing my actual symptoms, I am invited to look at them as messages with wisdom and valuable information—to listen and respond to.

～∽

*September, 1993 – June, 1994*
*Seattle*

## Slow Mend

I am weeping—rivers gush from my body, wracked loose in release. I cry for felled forests; for paved-over wetlands; for oil-slicked seabirds. Various scenarios of parched and poisoned earth take hold of me. No separation. Ingrid, my therapist, sits beside me, lifeline in the deluge. Her firm voice coaxes me back to myself. All this is in tracing where the wrenching pain in my heart originates from.

Through a series of sessions of dreambody dialogue, I slowly build up an understanding of etiology and cure. Since my first heart symptoms occurred in tandem with a vision, I trust that healing needs to come from that sphere. This is a slow process, under Ingrid's guiding care. It requires a shift in perspective—to listen to my symptoms, allowing that they are not the enemy, and ultimately to be instructed by their wisdom. Through this, I grow to understand that my heart is a delicate membrane pulsing in unison with the primal heart of the world; that I somehow risked obliteration by tapping into planetary despair. That, in the grand scale of that suffering, I was puny, my life negligible. I had been overwhelmed by a voltage beyond my heart's capacity to ground, leaving it unstable.

Week by week, in Ingrid's clear space of white-soft carpet and heaps of pillows, I learn that it isn't as simple as having one healing vision replace the devastation that I encountered, of existence sheared from source, during the Cairn of Mourning ritual. I see that a series of factors led up to my being susceptible in the first place, so the healing is an intricate process—constituted by grace more than anything, to move from Persephone as victim of abduction, to Persephone as Queen of the Underworld. I will learn to reign. Month by month in Ingrid's wide-windowed room—sunny days, cloudy days—looking out on a poplar-lined canal, I grow to understand that being abducted in the first place, assailed as I was by Earth's suffering, had everything to do with my naivety in invoking and encountering archetypal energies; with not having a strong sense of self to begin with; with having been abused myself at a stage of development when I needed to be securing boundaries; with giving myself away continually as an over-zealous mother. I become aware that all this was a set-up that left me defenseless.

Gradually, I grow to understand that if I can work with it, the same sensitivity that caused me to be struck to the core is potentially a gift. My wound becomes an ear, listening more deeply. Eventually what I hear must in turn be spoken. It becomes a bargain—if I live, I will tell. I will move from timidity into voice. I will learn to secure against dissolve and give expression to what I witness.

I will find that this work of healing, of being born into the whole, is a long labor, and the midwives are few. But it makes sense that to offset an accelerated heart, time needs to be taken—the art of the gradual, root word for "grail."

⁊

*Fall, 1993*
*Seattle*

## Dreambody Vision

*Heart failing, seeking healing, I journey North, to crystalline land stark-desolate and rugged. North to hard stone, to essence and only. North to vast expansiveness of those who came before and dwell in memory; who are memory, so easily forgotten and denied. Not of day vision, these eternal guardians of what remains after and only: grandmothers and great-grandmothers; great-great-grandmothers, through eras and ages, spanning generations. Shrouded, translucent, intimate with suffering, they gather round. Cedar Mother, ancient one, comes forward, leaning on her staff of living green. Her jade-green eyes peer into me, all-wise with an edge of daring. Compassion flows from her weathered clasp, firm-assuring through frail fingers.*

*By the fire circle, the ancestors gather round. Held in their embrace, my tears flow. Soft they whisper low in hush mur-murmuring as they encircle me, these wispy wizened ones. They already know of my foolish dabbling; of this shattered heart, too large now, endangered in having opened so to Earth's suffering extreme.*

*My tears flow for choked wellspring, for trees withering from sour rains; for the intrusions of roads; for the decimation of ancient groves. My tears flow for the absence of frog's song, the gaps of spe-*

*cies gone; for wetlands paved over, for blind material "progress." My tears flow for my children, for my children's children, for generations to come, deprived of fresh caress of breeze.*

*My weeping done, the ancient ones bow and depart; all except Cedar Mother.*

*In silence she leads me to an outcropping of stone, white-gray toned. Quartz? Marble? We bend down to an opening of rock face and enter an illumined cave. A path curves downwards, worn and smooth. Dark, but not entirely, light but not overtly. We walk, a spiraling path into the cavern depths. Cedar Mother hums a song in tenor droning. We come to an expanse where steam rises from a pool with the fragrance of vetiver, tree resin. At the water's edge, Cedar Mother gestures me to undress, to go in. I cast off dingy clothes—the burden of frayed travels that led me here, discarded.*

*Utterly weary, I slip into the water. The splash of entering echoes. Heart aching, heavy with grief, I sink into the warmth. Held by the waters, I slowly rise in a darkness luminous with song. My ragged breath deepens in this lull so close to sleep, so soothing. I float buoyant, submerged and merging, no boundary. Sorrow loosens, unraveling to dissolve into healing waters. A great shudder ripples through me, releasing the wound lodged at the center of my being. My heart becomes a pod-opening: petals enfolding core, sheaths of protection husking round.*

*I arrive in myself, no longer diffuse. Steady my heartbeat. No pain remains. Cedar Mother smiles as she chants. Radiant in joy now, aflourish with nourishing, all gnarls of anguish removed—her same sweet wise eyes shine through. Gratitude pulses within me. Oh, to breathe fully the yes of life*

*life life life!*

*Currents stream through in the surge of budding anew. Emerging I rise, a new fire kindled within, viridescent. Cedar Mother bows, lightly wrapping a cloak around me, woven of grasses and wildflowers. A tapestry of meadow enfolds me. She leads me back up the spiraling path, to the cave's mouth. We emerge.*

*A man of green waits there.*

*Have I not known him always, memorized his emerald gaze that sparkles now in recognition? With a cloak woven of leaves, a tapestry of forest, he stands majestic, crowned in sprouting vine. My heart swells beneath my folded hands. I move them to my side as he approaches. Bending down, he places his lips upon my breastbone to intone a long, low sound. A primal word I've known, yet have never heard aloud, vibrates within me. Its resonance enters and embeds within my heart. My wound becomes womb, nourishing this voice-seed that promises to come forth, bounteous and radiant in song.*

<hr />

*1993 – 1994*
*Seattle*

## Targeting the Heart

Alone in my bedroom, I take out the little boxes of Anthroposophical medicine from the pharmacy named after the archangel Raphael. This cosmic being of healing has also been known as Thoth, Hermes, and Mercury. He is keeper of the caduceus, the dynamic staff entwined with the symmetrical curve of two snakes, carried over from its ancient source to represent modern medicine. I trust the wisdom inherent in the research of spiritual science behind these medicines more than I do pharmaceuticals reduced to target the mechanism of disease. From each of the four boxes I take out one-gram glass ampules of clear liquid. They are scored where they narrow at the neck. I've done this enough now to know they break with a clean line. One by one, I tap the air bubbles out and then snap them open and with a fresh needle, draw in the clear liquid to fill the syringe. Then I plunge the needle sideways beneath my skin above my heart and press the plunger down. I've grown to appreciate this decisive action, of administering my own injections.

My prescription is a combination of potentized remedies that target my heart impairment on an energetic level. Through a highly refined process that hearkens back to my childhood hero, Paracelsus, original substances are repeatedly diluted and succussed (shaken in a prescribed manner) hundreds of times to arrive at their atomic imprint. Dr. Incao, with whom I consulted last summer, has tailored this particular combination to address my case, in consort with curative Eurythmy.

When I withdraw the empty syringe and needle, the entry point on my sternum swells a bit in the sting of healing. This taming of the wild drum of my heart is timed in consideration of cosmic rhythms, and how the body responds to them. For over a year I will repeat this subcutaneous penetration Sunday mornings and Wednesday evenings—five weeks on and two weeks off. Time is a loom where I weave my health in the tapestry of healing; this strand of medicine interweaves with curative gestures, with restorative images arising from body wisdom; a slow mend threaded through with grace.

*Spring, 1994*
*Seattle*

## Vessel of Transformation

On my bedroom door: a heart of gold gleams in greeting. It thuds gently when the door opens and closes, remarkably unbattered for how long it's dangled here. When it was first given to me, I sang "Heart of Gold," an old song, suddenly fresh—as if that croon of longing could be answered by a simple icon in a flash of daring; as if such searching could end here. I am mining for what will not tarnish.

As a homeopathic remedy, gold becomes cure for shrouded hearts in a mode closer to alchemy than chemistry, more in keeping with new physics than old science. Gold as original substance decreases in body yet increases in energy—potentized until no trace of original matter remains; atomic imprint strong.

*Aurum meticullum*—in accord with sun's radiance. I apply a salve of solar-heartedness. Sovereignty at the throne of being, at the core ... heart: coeur: courage, golden shield to deflect rather than merge.

I am apprenticed to this way of transformation. The golden heart hangs in a threshold place, a reminder of what endures. No one hears the slight knock it makes against the door. I'm busy here proceeding with working these last loads of lead through dissolve and dilution to eventual purification: a reconstellation in radiance, towards unwounded union.

*Summer, 1994*
*Bethesda, Maryland*

## Cardiac Consultation VI: New Prescription

In midlife, I am coming to terms with limitations that most people don't deal with until they reach old age. After a year of adjusting to my illness, I return to NIH. This check-up is en route to
England, where we are planning to live for a year since Atum has
been invited to assist in starting a master's program at a counseling
centre in London. No Brits have a Ph.D. in his field of transper-
sonal psychology, so working papers have been fairly easy to attain.
While Atum was off somewhere, I packed up the house with help
from my dear friend Geraldine, an honorary auntie to the kids. I
rented out our home of six years to someone we knew who agreed
to maintain it in our absence. Then I took off, kids in tow, stopping on the East Coast before flying overseas.

Back at NIH, I still fit the protocol for a pacemaker. Not
surprisingly, they still press for it since I haven't been doing so well
on the beta-blocker. I refuse again. The idea of a battery implanted
within me to electrically control my heart is menacing, a technological intimacy I'd never choose. They look at switching my
medication. I find out that if I had gone off the beta-blocker more
gradually, I wouldn't have experienced "rebound" and my heart
wouldn't have raced the way it did when I attempted to stop it.

Dr. L gives me the name of the top researcher in HCM in the
UK, Bill McKenna. "We don't see eye to eye on everything, but
he's doing major work," she says. Her idea is to give me a sample
of Verapamil along with a prescription, so that once I get settled in
England, I can go ahead and switch over, decreasing the Lopressor

gradually over two days, then starting in with the Verapamil. She complements me on being pretty astute as far as medical things go, but warns that most people would do this under medical supervision, and to go ahead and consult a doctor if I am so inclined. I thank her for the alternate drug and slip it into my purse.

*October, 1994*
*Sussex, England*

## Cardiac Consultations VII and VIII: Unremarkable Murmur

Rosy has begun kindergarten and it is the first time in many years that I do not have children home in the mornings. Embraced by the gently rolling hills of Sussex, where we are living now, I have begun to write, opening up to creativity in new and astonishing ways. I am writing a series of poems that articulate the imagery that came up in my therapeutic work around my heart. Through the process of giving voice, those subjective impressions become clearer. To give expression to the wisdom of my illness is a first touch into a potent magic. Through the act of bearing witness to this process, a shift is occurring: *I am no longer victim.*

On a Wednesday morning after dropping the kids off at school, I go to see a local GP to oversee my change in prescription so in case my heart races again, there is someone to call. His office is off a cobble-stoned courtyard of a centuries-old Tudor building, with hand-hewn beams and leaded glass wobbly in places. I explain the situation and he listens to my heart and suggests that I see a cardiologist to get some baseline tests done to monitor my heart. No pressure, only a recommendation. All I want to do is to change medication. I have always avoided unnecessary medical interventions, seeing technology for the most part as excessive. I certainly don't see that having an ECG for a new prescription is warranted. I am about to tell him so when a stillness fills the room, a grand pause. I notice the way the dust dances in the sunlight, coming in a shaft through the thick glass. Then, with the full intention of refusal, I open my mouth to say so but out of that deep silence a simple "yes" comes out instead. I have no idea why, but I have just agreed to go see another bloody cardiologist! I leave the appointment completely baffled by my uncharacteristic behavior. What is going on? Do I have some hidden desire for my cardiology file to grow thicker with more test results—some secret longing for more electrodes to be stuck on my chest?

A few days later, I finish up my series of heart poems. That evening I go to see the cardiologist in Crawley, a forty-five minute drive. I have good directions and find my way, even though I am still a bit off-kilter driving on the left side of the road. With my medical records in hand, I sit in the hospital waiting room, unsure of just what to expect.

After awhile, the cardiologist, Dr. S, comes out and introduces himself. He leads me back to the examination room. I notice a brightness about him, partly his bald head shining a bit, surrounded by sandy blond hair, and partly an eccentric emanation that comes with being devoted to investigation. We talk about HCM. He says there are 10,000 cases in the UK and downplays the fatality involved. He tells me that lots of genetic research is happening. It may seem futuristic, but they are working on a way to tell one's risk factor from a simple blood test. He asks me a slew of questions, scribbling away at his notes. Then he listens to my heart.

"A slight murmur," he concludes. "So the good old drug improved your condition. I think we should stay with it since it is proving reliable. However, the amount you are taking is enough to totally debilitate you."

I laugh in agreement. He continues, "Let's try cutting back on it and see how you respond." Then he sets me up for a standard electrocardiogram. Not relying on a technician, he lets me smear the gelatinous gunk and attach the electro-receptors myself, a participation that I appreciate. When the printout is done, he takes his time looking over my test results and then riffles through my records.

"Hmm," he murmurs. ·

Puzzled and intrigued, he grows more and more animated as he compares notes and asks me a new volley of questions about my original symptoms and subsequent diagnosis. His eyes grow brighter as he peers at me. "I am not sure what is going on here, but your test results simply don't match the characteristic presentation of HCM. Something is amiss." His enthusiasm reminds me of a genius scientist, with a touch of the eccentric, on the verge of discovery. "There is a mismatch here that just doesn't make sense. It doesn't fit."

Through the National Health Service, I was randomly assigned to Dr. S. It turns out that he works up at St. George's Hospital in London once a week with Dr. McKenna—the top researcher on HCM in the UK that I had heard about at NIH. Dr. S asks for permission to share my case with this expert, promising that he will get back to me about it soon. He tells me to start decreasing my Lopressor dosage by a quarter to begin with, saying there are no indications that I am at high risk for sudden death, and, "Sorry to say, no drug can prevent that anyway if it's going to happen."

He tells me, "You have an unremarkable murmur along with an unremarkable ECG." I know that this in itself is quite remarkable!

In the weeks following that consultation, there is an ecstatic feeling in my body in being released from the accustomed drag as I reduce the dosage of my daily medication. I don't need to sleep or rest so much. I hardly recognize myself when one night I wash the kitchen floor at 10 p.m. and am still chugging away. In a dream, I describe the lowering the medication, "It's as if you were told you have to live the rest of your life with the curtains drawn—and then, suddenly, they are thrown back and opened."

✑

*Spring, 1995*
*Sussex, England*

## Cardiac Consultation IX: Tilted Heart

Rooted here, in this land of my ancestors, a sense of belonging pervades me. Visceral. Grounding. A pace of life that allows for depth. Perhaps it is the scale of the village—we can walk most anywhere—the market, library, bank, post office, playground. Rhythm supported by culture. A balanced routine for my children, always a struggle to maintain in the hyper-hectic States, comes naturally here in the given regularity of the day: the tolling of the church bell up the hill marks the quarter-hours. Pause for morning coffee and afternoon tea. I have settled into a less rushed tempo. I can see how it has cultivated patience. This steady rhythm feeds my poetry and I am moving from skittering along the surfaces to a deeper rendering, drawing upon nourishment new to me, substantial. A relief.

I have been in England for five months now. Gradually I am meeting potential friends. I meet Marina in a craft circle, sewing little elvish felt slippers for a fundraising fair for the Waldorf school our children attend. Although her name means "of the ocean," Marina is very down-to-earth and sensible. In her early thirties, she is stretched between her osteopathic practice set up in her home and the demands of two young children and her artist husband.

Marina has insisted on driving me on this rainy evening for my appointment to meet Dr. S in Crawley to get the results from the definitive test that was taken at St. George's Hospital up in London a month ago. That was my fourth echocardiogram since I became a heart patient and I was surprised at how much time was spent on differing angles and having me hold my breath and switch my position. It took close to forty minutes. In the States, each test had been around five to fifteen minutes in all, quite cursory in comparison ("Technically marginal study" as stated in my NIH echo records.) During the sounding, various people came in, including Dr. McKenna, whom I didn't really get a good look at between the low lights and my immobile position, but he did introduce himself and I sensed his warmth and interest.

As we wait in the nondescript vinyl-seated waiting room in Crawley, I am not sure what to expect. Marina, having trained as a doctor, is familiar with hospitals and her chatting puts me at ease. Dr. S eventually comes out and greets me, then leads me back to the examination room. He is keen with fascination, with investigation. As soon as I sit down, he announces, "We knew from the beginning that you didn't have a straightforward case of HCM."

I nod, recalling his eagerness the last time I saw him.

"Now, your echo results were such that we weren't sure exactly what was going on ... "

I remember the researchers and doctors that clustered around the screen, examining and discussing my heart's proportions. I was curious about a certain angle being examined over and over again and the tone of intrigue in the words I heard murmured above me. Oblique. Obscure.

"We consulted with the top doctor in echocardiograms in the country—some say he's the best in the world, to interpret the results ... "

He pauses, to make sure I am following him.

"What we see here points to what I can only call a misdiagnosis ... "

I am taken aback, "How can that be?" I suggest that perhaps it has been healed. He doesn't quite scoff, but tells me that would be impossible.

He takes up a heart model and tilts it, demonstrating how it could be measured from an angle so that it would appear to be abnormally enlarged. He goes on to say that he guesses that the oblique nature of my heart had not been taken into account in my other tests. He tells me he'd really like to see my previous echoes, to compare them.

He suggests that I decrease the Lopressor gradually until I eventually phase it out altogether. Smiling broadly, he tells me to keep in touch if I have any symptoms. I thank him clumsily, stunned.

I return to Marina, who looks up from the paperwork she has brought along. She notices right away. "So?" she asks.

How do I tell her? A death sentence: lifted.

*Spring, 1995*
*Sussex, England*

## Solo

Where is Atum, my first husband, in these pages?

How do I show the choreography of distance? How we chose that dance in honing the independence each of us was molded by? A perfect fit.

How do I bring in the presence of absence?

Our marriage was an improvisation, never traditional, although it may have appeared so. My mothering was at the fore, my forte, my delight. I bow to that with gratitude. Atum and I turned away from one another increasingly until we had the courage to step outside of what originally held us.

⤳⤳

*Spring, 1995*
*Sussex, England*

## Cardiac Consultation X: "Spurious Diagnosis"

Transitioning off the medication hasn't been as easy or instantaneous as it first appeared it would be. After all, it's heavy-duty stuff. There have been ins and outs, ups and downs for a month now. I had a week from hell with back-to-back migraines and then episodes of shortness of breath, heart racing, and tightness in my chest when I exerted myself. Scary. I call Dr. S and he suggests that it might in fact be a valve defect, so the possibility of surgical replacement comes up again. He wants to see me to evaluate my heart murmur without the influence of medication, since I did have a mitral valve prolapse, which is common enough, but could have complications.

When I actually get to the appointment, the gradient of my heart murmur is slight; barely audible. In fact, I do not need a valve replacement after all. In fact, I have no irregular heart symptoms at the time for him to observe. Everything appears to be fine. It's a bit mysterious, and Dr. S says that there are some still unanswered questions.

Late the next afternoon, as I am making a cake for Rosy's fifth birthday party the next day, Dr. S calls. He tells me that he has spent the afternoon reviewing the tapes of my echo and is sorry to say that there is something "wrong" with my heart, "a gray area" he says, "certainly not as drastic as NIH communicated to you, but not clear either." The bottom line is that he doesn't feel qualified to define it and has set up a consultation directly with Dr. McKenna in a few weeks, up in London again.

A week later, I am walking with my new friend Celia, in the wet Sussex morning in the woods near her stone cottage. A strongly devotional "mum" in her late forties, she has a radiance about her, brighter than her golden hair. She is dedicated to her spiritual practice, which flows into her daily concerns with warm compassion and sweetness.

She is overseeing a massive renovation of their home. The first time I went there to meet her, she was going over plans for the bathroom to accommodate her older daughter, Mauni, born with spina bifida, which confines her to a wheelchair.

As we walk among bluebells, I share what is going on in the unfolding mystery drama of my heart. When I tell her the next step is to see Dr. McKenna, she very uncharacteristically interrupts me, "Dr. *Bill* McKenna?" she asks. When I say yes, she lets out a whoop. It turns out that this "big professor doc in his field," as she refers to him, is an old friend of hers and that Mauni worked as a receptionist in his office for a couple of years! Celia is excited to realize that his specialized work is related to my obscure condition.

Two weeks later, I return to St. George's Hospital accompanied by Celia. After a batch of tests, I meet McKenna, face-to-face. In a purple turtleneck and with an unmistakable majesty about him, he looks more like an orchestra conductor than a doctor. He beckons us to be seated at a round table. He begins by dramatically throwing down my batch of previous records. "Bizarre!" he exclaims. "I have to tell you this is as if I had been told that I would meet a three-foot small-bearded dwarf and instead in walks a six-foot tall human queen. That's how far off these previous tests are! There are huge discrepancies here, and it just doesn't make sense." And to make a point he jokes, "Are you sure these are the right records? Name? Doctor? Date?" He pages through the stack of papers. "Are you sure this is your file?"

I am impressed by his apparent centeredness and the serenity that radiates from him, no posturing of superiority or excitability and bafflement. Maybe it is having Celia there, but there is a relaxed atmosphere—not one I associate with medical situations. He turns to me, eye to eye, and asks directly, "What do you think is happening with your heart? Do you feel anything is wrong?" A deep question to be presented with, not unlike the healing question of the Grail story—*What ails thee?* The wounded king made whole and the wasteland restored through the compassion that flows through the act of asking. I tell him that I am rather mystified, but venture, "I believe I may have had the disease and have been healed." I don't dare to mention the how of it: remedies, healing images, and gestures.

He tells me in no uncertain terms that HCM is not something one can recover from and that from his point of view, a "spurious diagnosis" has been made. He tells me I am an example of someone who is a victim of doctors making things much worse. When he speaks of how my medication has been "zombie inducing," he enacts being hit over the head. I quite agree! He says that it has had such a dramatic effect on me because I didn't need it. Then he talks about today's tests results, all verifying that, "You do NOT have HCM, there is no doubt in my mind of that." He says that he hasn't been able to view the echo tape from NIH (since they have refused to release it) to see what they had seen, but his conclusion is that their diagnosis wasn't thorough and didn't take into account my angulated septum—the way my heart is tilted.

Besides the relatively common mitral valve prolapse, what shows up consistently is a depression in the sinus rhythm, which is usually no problem, although there is a 2% chance of complications. He says that the last test to be performed, to cover all bases, is a Holter monitor to watch that activity over a twenty-four hour period, but chances are it will be within the range of normal. He confides that "normal" is a lot broader than one would think, and there are many variations of the human heart. He tells Celia that their mutual friend Kathy has the same variation of sinus rhythm—and she recently climbed Mount Everest! He tells me to lead an active life, to do all that I've been holding back from, to go ahead and enjoy a new lease on life! Doctor's orders!

*Spring, 1995*
*London*

## Dancing Again

On the way home from my consultation with Dr. McKenna, I stop by at the National Gallery to see the paintings of Leonardo that I have always loved. I stand enraptured before his Virgin of the Rocks: mother goddess luminous within the depths of the Earth, her indigo mantle spread to encompass baby John with one arm, ushering him towards her roly-poly son, over which her other hand extends. She kneels, a bird just landed, yet entirely at home in crag and cavern, Madonna arising from stone. Beside her in the grotto, an angel smiles in demure tones. The painting, once an altar piece, resounds with gestures of blessing.

I find my way to the chapel-like room which houses Virgin and Child with St. Anne. I sit there and the tourists clear out, leaving me alone with the wall-size sepia sketch. Anne smiles radiantly as she enthrones her daughter, who reaches down to her son, who in turn reaches down to a lamb. I recognize a cascade of the same grace that moves in me. I let the miraculous settle in. "I am not a heart patient!"

I contemplate Dr. McKenna's words, "Mary, from now on I don't want you to even consider yourself to be a heart patient. It is important for you to let go of all the things you have been told by misled doctors. Don't identify with your previous diagnosis! It is simply flawed. All those things you were led to believe: they are just not you."

"I am not that diagnosis," becomes a meditation, a practice of disidentification of what has strongly defined me for the past year and a half.

Before catching the train back home, I find my way through back streets, letting the tension that I have been holding ease now and melt away. I gaze in the windows of galleries, bookshops, and cartographers. Where is a new map of my life without a disabling heart disease? An astonishing choreography that holds the promise: I will dance again!—and joyously so, as I grow accustomed to moving unhindered. I will inhabit my body in a new way, with a fierce sense of entering into life more fully than ever before, anchoring in a stout heart with no hesitancy.

> *Listen ~ seeds quicken;*
> *roots awaken as day ascends,*
> *subtle arousal*
> *potent with her song.*
> *The earth bears gold,*
> *Her belly glows with fire,*
>
> *I will dance a burning drum.*

❧

*Spring, 1995*
*Sussex, England*

## Gesture of Resurrection

I stand to look at my painting, a wet sponge in my hand. Carefully, I blot water onto the misshapen heart. Fluid once again, the red wakes up, becomes a vivid seep of blood. Wet on wet. Week after week, with curved strokes, I've re-wet this painting, brushing pigment in to shape the wash of carmine. I've had plenty of time to contemplate what my grandfather in a matter-of-fact way called my "impaired heart" while everyone else tiptoed around that fact.

Each painting session, I face the bulge and billow of my malformity: too big, too open. In layers of color and water, I have built up the form. My heart exposed upon the page.

Today, with recent news of my healing, it's time to add radiance to this rift. I dip my brush in golden yellow, and touch it to the page. Now the luminous gold merges with the red, suggesting flame. Gradually the heart becomes a vessel brimming with light. Slowly as I paint, following the wash of colors, a figure emerges from the ground of heart; arms outspread, stretching into an unexpected expanse—in the gesture of resurrection, set free.

~♀~

*May, 1995*
*Sussex, England*

## Heart's Song

Before our sojourn in England, when my hiking boots gathered dust, I had given them away. They had taunted me each time I encountered them in my closet, knowing my heart was too weak for me to use them. Or so I had thought. So, now that I could hike again, getting a new pair to wear—and use!—was cause for celebration. I found a pair of leather "Eurohikers," sturdy and supportive, brown with purple laces. My new footwear was inaugurated in an auspicious hike with Annie, in the first of many climbs to come.

Annie and I had met in a writing class when we both wrote similar pieces expressing our love for trees. Lion-maned, her wild reddish hair made mine seem tame since it wasn't as long or corkscrewy as hers. Her delicate face bespoke an intense sensitivity that

I would come to know along with her strengths of laughter, insight, unmistakable warm-heartedness, and a sense of the sacred. It turned out that she had been the representative in Scotland for "Children of the Green Earth" and there were many other synchronicities that flowed between us.

This first real hike taken with my heart sound again is a pilgrimage of sorts. Annie takes me along to participate in the project she is doing as a culmination of a voice training. It involves singing to the trees at the height of the Downs (the Downs are actually up, being a range of soft rolling hills that once held an inland sea). After a lengthy drive, we meet six other women friends of hers, mostly fellow students in her course, in a car park at the bottom of the mount.

We walk on the chalky paths in gradual ascent, chatting some, in silence at times.

I recognize that lark's trill in the chattering of birds. It takes us over an hour to climb up to our destination: Chanctonbury Ring. Known as the "Monarch of Sussex Hills," this site was once an old Roman hill fort and a Celtic-become-Roman temple dedicated most recently to Diana, Venus and Flora. These three, as Greek goddesses—Artemis, Aphrodite, and Persephone—are ones I honor for their respective qualities of intimacy with nature, love and the soul, qualities that sustain me and will prove to be a keynote of solidarity with Annie over the years.

I delight in my newfound stamina as we reach an open space at the top, where light breezes are blowing. A ring of beech trees once stood here, centuries old. In the hurricane of '87 most of them were blown down, as were millions of trees across England.

Their uprooting here had unearthed ancient pottery preserved amidst their roots.

In this place of ruin and restoration, we find a secluded spot by a remaining monarch beech tree on the hillside. Stepping through scrub, we come to encircle its deeply creased elephantine bark. Annie leads us and our song goes out from our circle to the few beech elders nearby that have been spared, as well as to the newly planted trees. Following Annie's example, deep croonings arise from us in a weaving of harmonies: lamentation, joy, and praise. My heart is radiant with song, pouring forth with a force far beyond words, call it kinship, good will, love. My pulse becomes one with the trees, a shared circulation.

That night, I sleep soundly, grateful for exertion and vigor. My victory.

❧

*Autumn, 1995*
*Sussex, England*

## Story Fire

We originally planned to stay in England for only a year. However, Atum has been invited to extend his teaching at the counseling centre in London. Although our marriage is withering (and that is another story), it is a blossoming time for him professionally. He is teaching extensively on the continent and his work with men's issues is becoming increasingly popular. Since he was never one for being at the home front, Sussex provides as good a base as any for his traveling-teaching. The kids missed the States at first, but are settling in. We decide to stay, and will end up there four years in all.

I am delighted for a number of reasons. I feel a resonance with the land itself, and the scale and quality of life here seems ideal for raising children. The staidness of rural England is balanced with the fact that Forest Row is an international community built around the various trainings that, along with Waldorf education, have grown out of Anthroposophy. I enjoy stepping into "Seasons," the local health food store down the lane from us, where I hear people speaking different languages while I choose vegetables from local biodynamic farms. This rural setting is far more culturally diverse than anywhere we've lived before. When I sign up for a storytelling training at Emerson College, out of a group of twenty students, sixteen countries are represented!

In the storytelling training, to choose our first substantial stories to work with, we randomly draw from an anonymous pile of Wonder Tales spread face down on the floor. I am appalled to end up with the Old Russian "Vassalisa the Brave." I expected the realm of "Wonder Tale" to be all sweet enchantments and loveliness and here I am with a fierce and dreadful hag! An innocent girl is thrown out by her cruel stepmother into the wild forest to fetch light from a terrible witch. Baba Yaga's devouring hostility is chillingly vivid to me. As the girl becomes her servant under threat of being the next meal, I fall captive in that hut surrounded by its fence of bones. The lanterns set on every post are human skulls.

This story constellates for me the Hungarian refugee, Magda, who lived with my family of origin for a decade and "cared" for me from when I was three weeks old, while my mother worked full-time. Having just escaped the Russian invasion at eighteen, which included witnessing people run over by tanks and her friend jump out a window, Magda was traumatized and given to fits of rage.

This included violence against me. I worked with the ramifications of that abuse in the safe container of psychotherapy years ago. Still, those incidents are entrenched in me, a deep clamp upon setting my voice free.

Baba Yaga rides her mortar and pestle across the sky with dawn, day and night at her command. Hers is the domain of death, certainly. I can barely stand working with the confrontation with the Dark Mother at the heart of the story. I come near to giving up more than once. But I trust in the power of archetypal story to bring resolution. "Vassalisa the Brave" does end happily after all. I persist and eventually find fierce voice in Vassalisa's victory. I learn how to return to the land of the living without being devoured.

On campus, there is a tulip poplar tree that I am particularly drawn to. In the spring, I marvel at the miniscule newborn leaves already in the four-lobed shape of full grown leaves. I am delighted to learn that it was planted by Richard St. Barbe Baker, the visionary forester who had founded Children of the Green Earth at the end of his life. I am continuously amazed that he was responsible for the planting of twenty-six trillion trees! This gives me hope in the power of restoration. I have known my heart to be intimately related to the Earth's suffering; now I turn to emphasize its association with regeneration.

As I move deeper into the full-time transformative training, I recognize that storytelling is a natural development of my involvement in ecological restoration. In Deep Ecology, the primary ritual of the Council of All Beings is based on a deep listening that leads to speaking for something in the more-than-human world (i.e., animal, plant, or landscape). One extends one's identification to a particular aspect of nature and, from that awareness, tells its story. Working intensively with story opens me to this birthright of every human being that has become obliterated by modern culture. Primed to be in communion with a richly storied world, we can reclaim that dynamic relationship.

I research an Aboriginal myth that honors the creative force of stories and how intertwined they are with sustaining the living Earth; how imperative it is for humans to rekindle this power. I shape my own version of this wise tale from a production of Omega Theater in Boston, which I call "Story Fire," elaborating on a basic sketch.[2]

This story provides a context for the mandate of storytelling. It's been a couple of years now since the ritual work I led when my heart had broken. As a part of the culmination of the storytelling training, I lead a simple version of the Council of All Beings, using my telling of "Story Fire" to set the tone and context. The ritual is warmly received by my fellow students, who enjoy the opportunity for spontaneous storytelling.

Enacting The Council again makes me intensely aware of my melancholic nature, my penchant for grief. Because of the dire state of the planet, of course this makes sense. Joanna Macy's "Despair and Empowerment" work is based on the need to break through denial and open up to the depths of despair resulting from our interconnectedness to the suffering of the world. That despair fuels one to take action on behalf of the living Earth. This is understood as the complementary force to grief. Now I discover another counterpart: the profound human capacity to give praise. I realize how I overdid the lamentations and omitted this necessary element of celebration, which in being a creative act, is another level of empowerment. Alleluia!

It is not a small order for me to let go of my presiding belief that humans are primarily a destructive force wreaking havoc on the planet. I shift focus to include the value of human life—to not only be a part of the web of life in all its facets of interconnectedness, but to acknowledge that wholeness and give gratitude for it as well.

> *The earth—ah, who knows her losses?*
> *Only one who with nonetheless praising sound*
> *Would sing the heart, born into the whole.*
>                     —Rainer Maria Rilke[3]

I lead several more Councils with Duncan, my storyteller friend/colleague, accompanying me with his beautiful djembe drum, since I am rather timid at drumming in any substantial way myself. I use Story Fire as a centerpiece for these rituals and bring in a new emphasis on praise to engender a sense of hope. One Council takes place in the basement of St. James Piccadilly, the church where William Blake was baptized. It is odd to not have access to nature as a direct source of inspiration, but it still works, using imaginative visualization.

Another Council of All Beings takes place over a weekend in Cornwall by the ancient healing well of Sancreed, where ribbons are tied to a grand old hawthorn tree beside stone steps that descend down to the spring. One evening, a couple who comes to the workshop invites us to their farm for dinner and a bonfire. They bring out boat-size drums hollowed out of enormous tree trunks, up to my chest and four to six feet in circumference. That night in the blaze of firelight, I stand above a massive tree-become-drum and feel my way into the group rhythm. Rooted in the Earth below, not far from ancient standing stones, I overcome my wavering and found a steady beat that I can trust. On all of these occasions, my heart remains steady, another reason to praise.

*In the beginning, Tiawa, the Great Spirit, created the whole world by telling stories, so every being had a story to tell. But, there was no one to listen to them. So Tiawa created Sajecho, whose name means the voice of the Earth and Sotaknang, the giver of visions as her partner. Sajecho listened to all living things—both visible and invisible—and filled with their stories, she told them to Sotaknang with great joy. As she spoke, her words came to life. So were born the people of the story, who were given magical tongues, so each time they told their stories, the stories were new and different, but always resonant with truth.*

*As long as the people of the story retold their tales, the voices of Sajecho and Sotaknang spoke wisdom to their hearts. As long as they retold their stories, the people lived in harmony with the kingdoms of nature: mineral, plant, animal and in peace with one another. They lived in accord with the nature spirits and heavenly beings. Yes—every bird, beast, fish and insect; the mountains, rivers, trees and little flowers—each had its place around the story fire.*

*And so it continued, generation after generation.*

*But gradually the people drifted away from the Story Fire. Villages became towns and towns became massive cities. They were cut off from source, and even time became straightlined to them. They conquered the Earth and all her creatures to satisfy their needs. But no matter how much they took, it was never enough—they always wanted more! Great forests were felled to the ground; great rivers laid to waste; even the once-sweet air was fouled. The peoples' lives had become a wasteland as well, filled with manufactured things, busyness* and noise. Even silence was endangered. They could no longer hear the voice of Sajecho in their hearts and the visions of Sotaknang inspired them no more. They became spectators of a cool light that replaced the original hearth of story. But it didn't matter to them. In their frenzy, they didn't notice what they were missing. Little by little, many stories of Sajecho were forgotten and the ones that remained were scoffed at and called foolish. Only a few elders kept the stories, but no one cared to listen.

Without being honored, the elements were estranged. Without their stories being told, Eagle, Coyote, Mountain Lion, and Deer and all their brothers and sisters no longer came to the story fire to listen or dance.

The story circle was broken. The fire was reduced to embers and ash.

Eventually, without their stories being told, the rain ceased to fall and the wind stopped blowing. When the people saw this, they grew afraid. They sought out the elders who told them that the sun would not rise in the morning without its story being told, and that when the last story was forgotten, the Earth itself would be gone. The elders told them that Sajecho had not forgotten: still she sang to the peoples' hearts and they could find her voice embedded within them. And so they did. First it came in dreams—and then, little by little, they found their way back to attend to the old stories, and to tell them once again. And they found new stories, resonant with truth, as well.

When Rain heard its story being told, it began to fall, and breezes stirred in the still air when Wind's story was mentioned. One by one as they were invited back, all the birds and beasts and spirits of Nature came to gather around the people who were remembering them. The story circle was mended, the story fire tended, all the more lovingly in *returning to it. From that ancient yet new fire, many stories are being lit to bring warmth and light to these leaden times.*

*So, people of the story, find silence and listen deeply: What part of creation, visible or invisible, is waiting to tell you its story? Listen deeply and bring that story to life.*

∾

*Fall, 1997*
*Devon, England*

## Rubedo

As our time in England drew to a close, I was able, through serendipity and grace, to attend a course called "Wild Mind." It was held at Schumacher College, a premier institute for ecological studies located in Totnes, in Devonshire. Generations of my ancestors had lived nearby in the village of Ashburton, bordered by windswept heaths with granite tors. In the flowing slopes of Devon, we put pen to page to express how place had shaped us, to evoke home or lack of home, to provide a testament to nature.

*Text of mountain, voice of wind, phrase of forest, echo of river.*

The potency in being there, essentially on retreat, made up for the deficiency of inwardness of my past decades. In my dorm room, I put up a drawing of a white horse that my daughter had drawn, evoking her tender presence in the empty room. Every evening, from a red phone booth in the courtyard, I spoke to my kids at home. Every morning it felt odd to awaken with only myself to prepare for the day, only my own bowl to fill. I spent time in solitude in the woods, delighting in my first encounter with the scent of ivy blossom, soul-searching about all the ways my marriage had gone wrong and still believing that we could fix it.

I began an apprenticeship to the way of *rubedo*, the red stage in alchemy devoted to passionate engagement. On that ancestral ground, I began to understand that we are all broken, that for me the way of healing has everything to do with opening through our brokenness to wholeness despite all the ravages. I began to see that healing can be nothing more—or less—than continuing to love the living Earth, and to bear witness to her myriad wonders, despite all that is waged against her—against us as part of her.

It was time to leave the village life I had become accustomed to, time to take the mended drum of my heart into the tattered world.

॰॰॰

*November, 1998*
*Seattle*

## Urban Return

We return to live in Seattle again, to the house we bought a decade ago. New building is happening everywhere. More people crowd the park. Traffic has increased and backs up in the busy streets nearby. I find our old grandmother clock silent, in need of repair. A weight has fallen and broken through the bottom. It has been unwound these past four years and is full of cobwebs. Its hands are frozen in place at twenty past four and the dial at the top of the clock face that keeps the moon phases is stuck on the clipper ship of "no moon."

I clean it out, polish the dark wood until it shines. I have it repaired so now the chimes call out, every fifteen minutes, the way the church bells do in Forest Row. This clock, running smoothly now, is my ally in reentering this place of acceleration—keeping rhythm, keeping time. A reminder. My pace has quickened. I am getting accustomed to the fragmentation that comes from hours of driving and shuffling kids far and wide (they each attend a different school and their social lives are expanding)—glimpsing majesty on the horizon, just out of touch, all autumn's glory flashing by my car window. American voices become familiar again—loud, crass. It seems as if everyone around me is on speed (or is it just coffee?). How long until I start moving at the same frantic pace?

*Summer, 1999*
*Seattle*

## Hera Chera

Driving home from a legal consultation to file my divorce from
Atum, I switch on the radio ... "severely parched land" reported
from Greece. On Samos, fires are blazing out of control. Hera's
island is burning. Evacuations are taking place. I, too, am fleeing
her sacred ground of matrimony and betrayal, leaving a marriage
long arid, my heart brittle, hidden too long.

My bridal veil was fine antique mesh from my grandmother's
drawer, gathered to a crown where I wound lilies of the valley
round with satin ribbon. There are so many veils in marriage. Fila-
ments weave transparency, obscurity, cocoon, encasing. We con-
ceal and reveal ourselves. Lace, membrane, gauze, net.

I always avoided Hera, shunned her story. What was there
to tell? Her bitter glory of wifeness? Her wrath and vindictiveness,
her perpetual victimization? She appears in a recitation of reaction, of cruel revenge. Does it bear repeating?

But before the Hellenes, her cult celebrated sexuality as potent
as what became Aphrodite's domain. Hera Talaia: fruitful ephiph-
any, marriage as true union, beyond its contraction into contract.

Reduced to figures and furnishings, we divide the marital
community. "Dissolution" it's called in the state of Washington,
and what was that phrase: Irretrievably broken? Irreparable? Beyond reconciliation. I left the documents behind, but not Hera.
She's been stalking me. She doesn't care about the rightness of
wording; she knows this is no abrupt severing. She knows it is akin
to famine in her world, parched land.

My marriage lasted twenty-two years, more than half my life, but I'll outgrow that if I'm lucky. These first steps of walking away mark a road ahead that I welcome.

Hera's luck is that she has a hidden side, another aspect beyond heavenly queen and bride. *Wife* doesn't contain her. Hera Chera: She Who Turns Away. Waning moon, dark moon. Her adamancy for true union, not fully met, turns to seeking solitude.

Veil becomes shroud.

In the guise of marriage, I was wed to isolation. I disguised absence, holding out for change. So many ways I hid in the shell of marriage, cracked open now. This is the change I held out for: shedding a form outworn. Turning away, walking away, leaving. I tear away the veils, strip away the shrouds. My heart sounds a note of new beginning, unknown dance on scorched terrain.

⁊⁊

*July, 1999*
*Bethesda, Maryland*

## Cardiac Consultation XI: Coyote in the Corridors

I've traveled with my kids from Seattle to the East Coast for a family reunion and have arranged to spend a morning going out to the HCM clinic at NIH, where I was last seen eight years ago. I want the docs to know how things have turned out, that their echoes were a fluke, a "spurious diagnosis" ... that I have been off the debilitating drugs for seven years with no problems. I believe that my case has something to offer to their research, something important for them to make note of, considering how dire my situation was before.

I walk up the steps from the subway into the sweltering morning, carrying a book about Coyote, the trickster, that I just began reading on the ride out to this suburb of D.C. As I ascend, I can't help but recall my last visit here: how I faltered and paused to catch my breath in the few blocks to the clinical center. It had been a landmark for my new identity as an invalid to discover how walking even a short way was an effort, especially when compounded by the heavy humidity. I am here again, in the same oppressive heat, but I am walking at a clip now, buoyed by the victory of having my health. Little had I expected, then, to return with such a stride! I can't help but smile.

I find my way through the mega medical campus to the largest building of all, the Clinical Center. The magnitude of this place is still imposing, even if I do have good news. The cardiac clinic on the fifth floor looks vaguely familiar, although it's empty at this early hour. I go up to the young man at the receptionist's desk. "Hi, I'm Mary. I have a seven o'clock appointment."

Barely looking up from his computer screen, he dictates in monotone, "ECG, first floor, the lab is to your right after you get off this elevator. Then come back up here for an echo."

"But wait—I don't need to have any tests done. I came to go over my case with the doctors here."

He riffles through a folder, then mutters, "Tests first. It's on this chart. They won't see you until they have the results." He hands me my file.

"Hold on—I'm a former patient and I just wanted to talk to the doctors about my situation."

"Yes, you're on the schedule, but you got to do the tests before you see anyone—that's how it goes." He returns to the keyboard. I know I am being dismissed. This isn't quite what I had expected, but they must need data to discuss. Oh well. I go down to the ECG lab. They are ready for me. The sophisticated machines are smaller than I've known before, with computer printouts of the squiggly lines; nifty, quiet, and fast. Before I know it, the technician rips off my copy. "There you go, take that back up to the clinic with you. You can put the robe in that bin."

As he leaves, I thank him. Disrobing, I glance down at my readout. It has my name, along with a long patient ID number. Then below: "ECG, abnormal." I peer closer. There is the squiggle of my sinus rhythm variation, again.

I return to the clinic and wait to be called for my echocardiogram. What few windows there are look out on brick walls. In the echo room, I am led to a little cubicle with a cot and what appears to be a PC on steroids. With a forced smile, the petite technician introduces herself—"I'm Pamela"—as she shoves a gown into my hands. "Here you go." Then she rapidly draws the curtains around me and the humming machine and makes a phone call, full of exasperation. After changing, I sit looking at the blank screen, overhearing her complaints about her air-conditioning at home not working. I wait. And wait, reading a bit more about Coyote, the trickster deity, until Pamela finally yanks open the curtains and begins brusquely to attach adhesive pads to my chest, saying, "Okay, let's get going here."

As she begins to connect the leads to the little snap-shaped metal extrusions, I tell her, "Before you start, I wanted to let you know that I saw a HCM research doctor in England and had a really substantial echo done with him overseeing it. They took forty-five minutes to do my echo and found that my heart was tilted.

They think that this gave the impression of HCM, but it was actually the way it is positioned."

Scowling down at me, she replies, "Look, this is my job. I know how to do it!" In a huff, she changes the subject, "I hear that everyone drinks coffee in Seattle ..." and proceeds to perform a precursory echo. The Doppler sound of my heart accompanies the various views on the screen: cross sections, measurings. Before I know it, she is ripping the electrode stick-ons off. Not gently. "We're done in here."

The waiting room has filled up. There is a mother and her son, who looks to be about ten years old. Gently, she is telling him, "Mommy needs to get heart surgery." I recognize her stoic bravery and wonder what it means to him. Here I am, in a room of heart patients. I ponder what stories live beneath each waiting face. I open my book to Coyote, whose motto is: Things are not what they seem.

*When Coyote is around there is going to be trouble, and often trouble of the ridiculous sort ...*[4]

After many pages of the ever-changing trickster, a nurse— Carol—calls my name, and I go back to be examined: weight, blood pressure, a listen to my murmur. When she gets to inquiring about my symptoms, I tell her why I am here, how I actually don't have HCM. She dutifully notes my experience with no response, and proceeds to ask me a battery of standard questions:

"Shortness of Breath? Fatigue? Light-headedness? Blackout? Chest Pain? Palpitations? High Pulse? "

I enjoy answering "no" to all the symptoms of HCM, right down the line. "No."... "No." ... "No." ...

When she is done, she excuses herself. "Okay, if you would just wait here. I'll need to confer with the doctor and get back to you."

Waiting, I bring out my book companion.

*A trickster does not live near the hearth; he does not live in the halls of justice, the soldier's tent, the shaman's hut, the monastery. He passes through each of these when there is a moment of silence, and he enlivens each with mischief, but he is not their guiding spirit. He is the spirit of the doorway leading out.*

I wait. Carol returns to say, "The doctor would like to arrange an MRI for you in order to get a closer look at your heart. This is an outpatient procedure but it would require that you spend the day here. I can set something up for this afternoon over at Veteran's Hospital." I know from Philip Kilner, a cardiology researcher in England who works with this kind of imaging, that it provides more accuracy than echocardiograms. But as appealing as it is to have an MRI on the house, I don't have the time. I let her know that I appreciate the offer, but I have children to return to and a train to catch to Philadelphia in the midafternoon.

An opportunity obscured.

She nods, "Okay then, you can return to the lobby. The doctor is in cardiac cath but he has requested to see you personally. You are next up for a consultation. Have a seat. We'll get back to you."

I go and wait again. Coyote and me.

*Coyote is the spirit of the crossroad at the edge of town. He is the spirit of the road at dusk, the one that runs from one town to another and belongs to neither. There are strangers on that road, and thieves, and in the underbrush a sly beast whose stomach has not heard about your letters of safe passage.*

Finally, at close to eleven o'clock, Carol, the nurse returns. "Thank you for waiting. The doctor is available. This way ... " She leads me down a long corridor, past all the rooms I had been in already, to a new one. From the other end, the bleached figure of a white-coated man comes closer—close enough for me to see his dark, ruffled hair, his blazing eyes: *The* doctor. In deference to him, Carol steps back to be beside me, introduces us, "Dr. Fananapazir." He shakes my hand in an agitated way, "Pleased to meet you again."

With quick strides, we come to a conference room, where four of his colleagues, all in uniform white coats, await us. Seated at an imposing table are Pamela, the echo technician, and then Fananapazir's assistant, Dotti, along with another nurse and researcher who are briefly introduced to me. Carol indicates a seat, and sits down across from me, joining everybody else, who is lined up on either side of Dr. Fananapazir. I am alone at the other side of the table, facing them. More a trial than a consultation!

"Well, I hate to be the bringer of bad news, but you need to know that there is absolutely no question that you have a case of Obstructive Hypertrophic Cardiomyopathy! All your test results show this." Dr. Fananapazir clicks on a switch to show a frame from my echo, projected on a screen. He slams a pointer against the image, "Look here. This is your septal muscle! See this?" and he calls out the measurements. "Now, I am sorry to be the bringer of bad news," he repeats, "but this is proof that you have HCM. This is not a subtle diagnosis! How dare McKenna suggest that there is no evidence of hypertrophy!"

There is enmity towards McKenna and impatience towards the bother of it all. Sensing a rivalry with McKenna, I ask,

"Have you ever met Dr. McKenna?"

"Why, yes—at conferences," he fumes. "We often cross swords."

I have become another sword between them. Crossed. I need to summon a shield for myself. I take a deep breath, trying to dispel the pervading intimidation of being opposed by this team. Trying to prevent my voice from quavering, I venture, "I came to see you again because I thought that you would be interested to learn that I have been fine now for seven years, off of the medication you prescribed. When I was here before, I was told that my symptoms would never change and that I would need to be on medication forever."

"Yes, ... well," he stammers. "It's a ... a ... variable disease."

Then he continues, "You realize that because this is a hereditary condition that your children are at risk. We are on the cutting edge of research. This is our field. We are tracking families. In the future, there will be a simple genetic test to see who may be at risk. We would be happy to follow your children here, anytime you want to bring them to see us. They can arrange it at the front desk of the clinic."

He goes on, "Remember that you are still eligible for a pacemaker from us, so keep that in mind. Your children will most likely qualify for pacing as well."

I return to my question of being off medication for seven years with no symptoms. He evades it again. We are enacting a strange repetition and refusal to listen. In frustration, I finally turn to his assistant and ask, "Is there research on cases where there is no symptomatology? Have you seen this before?"

She looks shocked that I would address her and shoots a look to him. "Doctor?"

He nods to her and says, "Well, this is a dynamic disease. Now, the symptoms are one thing, and sudden death is another. In your case there is a lower probability of that risk. On a one-to-ten scale, you are probably a three. It is in your favor that there is no family history behind you of sudden death. Others are not so fortunate." His voice lowers as he declares his final word. He looks at his watch as he rises to his feet. Everybody else stands and I follow suit, lapsing behind them. He gives me one last glance and, whoosh, he is gone.

His assistant comes over to me and gives me her card. "Here is my contact information, if you want to pursue finding out about the research."

"Thank you." I say, as we all walk out of the room.

I clutch the Coyote book in my hands, my only ally.

Absolutely unaware of my own inability to listen, these five hours at NIH seem to be a waste of time—my case certainly didn't have the impact I had hoped it would. Later, I discover that huge controversies have raged around Dr. Fananapazir for years. I take this all as confirmation of my inclination to discount him. Why should I respect his opinion when it has been openly refuted by some of his own colleagues?

❧

*August, 1999*
*Seattle & Olympia*

## Unexpected Call

In the scorching morning, I am driving south out of Seattle to take my eldest son Chris to see a cardiologist. I have dropped Rosy off to spend the day at a friend's. As soon as I am alone in the car, a wavering moves through me. *Is his heart okay?* What will this doctor's visit reveal? Interstate 5 is at its worst, gritty and noisy with construction delays. I need to keep the windows open for air. My old wobbly-wheeled Volvo is out of sync with the speedy interstate. The faster I go, the more the car shimmies. I pull over to see if I have a flat, but the tires seem fine. I'm not, though. No matter how mellow the music in the tape deck is, it doesn't sooth me. My shoulders are tense, my jaw clenched. But my shakiness is matched by my determination to be strong.

When he called from his home in Olympia last week, I knew right away that he was not okay. Over the phone, he told me how his heart was "doing this weird *ba-boom* thing sometimes and I can feel it kind of jump out of my chest." I (calmly) suggested going to see a doctor to get it checked out. The results of his first ECG, which measures the electrical activity of the heart in waves and rhythms was defined as "abnormal," with arrhythmias. Next step: cardiac consultation, which led to an echocardiogram. His first, of course. Today we return to the cardiologist to hear the results.

I had put aside the threat of genetic heart disease looming over my offspring when I was told I didn't have HCM. What can this be? I want to drop everything to support Chris in dealing with unaccustomed heart symptoms, not to mention doctors. Not that I have any idea of how to express this to my twenty-one-year-old son who is busy establishing his independence. I make it known that I am there for him. What else can I do?

I pick Chris up at the house that he shares with other Evergreen College students and we find our way to the mega-clinic

again. We walk from the shade-covered parking lot to the sprawl-
ing complex of medical buildings. Chris hasn't had any more
symptoms since the day he called me. He's always been relatively
healthy, so this is all new to him: the long wait in the cardiology wing decorated in over-cheer, the numerous charts, the white
coats, the rolling medical equipment.

As we sit in underlying tension, Chris, as usual, applies his
wry wit to politics and tells me of his latest reads. Although he is a
bit bothered about having to deal with seeing a doctor, his capacity
for intellectual fascination isn't at all diminished. In the midst of
researching revolution and brimming with enthusiasm, he tells me
all about a radical historian he has recently discovered.

We are finally taken back to meet Dr. Y, I notice his full
moon-face again, not unlike Chris's. New in the practice, he is
cordial, stiff with his own agenda. At the consultation last week,
he rushed through the medical history. I tried to explain about my
misdiagnosis, but he hardly listens. In the notes I read later, I will
find he refers to my condition as "Hypertensive Cardiomyopathy" which may have been a clerical error, or confusion, for of the
seventy-five names for HCM, this one doesn't exist.

In the windowless room, Chris sits quietly, shifting his weight
from time to time in the molded plastic chair while I take notes.
In his thick Chinese accent, Dr. Y rushes through the results of
the echocardiogram taken a few days ago. He says that Chris has
indications of "ASH" and, without pausing, offers to give him
a prescription.

"Wait a moment … " I interject, "Can you tell us more
about ASH?"

"It's short for Aseptal Hypertrophy … " he says.

I recognize the word for enlargement. But when I ask, Dr. Y says it isn't HCM at all, that we just need to watch, that Chris's tachycardia incident could well have been stimulated by alcohol and he should avoid drinking and caffeine. He returns to the offer of a beta-blocker. "But why should he take that if he's not having any symptoms and hasn't had any since that one incident?" I ask, indignant.

Shrugging, Dr. Y responds, "Well, most people just like to take something. It makes them feel safer."

Out of view of the doctor, Chris rolls his eyes at me. I nod, slightly. We leave without a prescription, without a picture of this diagnosis, without a sense of its possible consequences. We leave without safety, but relieved not to be grabbing onto pills, simply for the sake of it.

✌

*May, 2000*
*Seattle*

## Anomaly

Driving Emmanuel to get an echocardiogram, we mostly spoke about plans for his upcoming high school graduation. With dutiful mother overview, I had taken stock of what he might need before leaving home. What holes were left in his upbringing? He was pretty good in the kitchen, and I was showing him how to balance a checkbook. He applied to Evergreen College and was accepted, along with a grant for his excellent GPA. He did well in school without being really turned on to a particular subject. I often had the sense that he was waiting to be ignited.

Since Hypertrophic Cardiomyopathy is a hereditary disease, I had been told that all my kids should be screened when their hearts were fully grown at eighteen, Emmanuel's age now. I had let that go when I received a clean bill of health. But now I was again facing the searing prospect of congenital heart disease in my other children. Best to have him checked before he moved out.

That was my first time back to Zenith Cardiology in eight years. We were led to a corner room with windows on both sides. The sun streamed through the new green of birch trees blending its rays with the already bright fluorescent light. Once the echocardiogram was underway, Luke, the technician, lanky with salt-and-pepper hair and wire-rim glasses, started telling me what we were seeing. In the language of blood volumes and hemodynamics, he pointed out the threefold tricuspid valve, pulsing from above, and then the vena cava. He was animated as he guided me through the various views and measurements, obviously turned on to his work. The amplified heartbeat was constant behind our conversing. Then he fell silent and the only sound in the room was the telltale *ba-boom, ba-boom, ba-boom* of Emmanuel's heart. Luke's demeanor shifted as he became intent on replaying the same image, again and again. He grew pensive. Then he asked, "Emmanuel, do you play sports?'

"Some basketball, but I am not on a team or anything."

"What kind of exercise do you do?"

"I walk three miles a day."

"Hmm. Well this is showing that your right atrium is a bit enlarged. Sometimes we find that in athletes. I don't think walking would warrant it."

A cloud went over the sun. The room dimmed, became colder.

Luke told me he wanted to see if there was a cardiologist on duty that he could catch to look at the test. He left the room.

Emmanuel and I looked at one another, puzzled. I had to work at keeping alarm at bay and made an effort to steady my breath. Soon Luke returned with a woman in a snow-white coat with a stethoscope dangling around her neck. She warmly shook my hand and nodded to Emmanuel. "Hi. I'm Dr. H. Let's take a look at what is going on here." She moved in close to watch the screen.

Ten minutes later, another test was underway to more carefully trace the blood flow through Emmanuel's heart. Induced with a saline solution, air was bubbling through his veins, Dr. H invited me to come up close to look at the screen. She pointed out the area to watch at the top of the septum. "There!" she cried out as a little blip went from left to right. Almost simultaneously, Luke aha-ed in recognition.

"It's not supposed to go that way." Dr. H said, as she pointed to miniscule whirls on the screen. Just as I focused in, another swirl danced across. She exclaimed again, "There. That was a big one. Did you see that?" I had. A bubble had burst through, from one side of his heart to another, where there should be no way to get through.

"Yes," I replied. I looked at Emmanuel. I sensed his breathing change, ever so subtly becoming shallower. Our eyes met across the room, seeking reassurance. His glance had the same probe and startle I knew from times of danger.

"So we see that the membrane is not intact." Dr. H directed the nurse to stop injecting the solution. Then she gently explained that in order to know more, we would need to do a more conclusive echocardiogram, a TEE—taken through the esophagus, with sedation, to give a clearer picture of the anatomy of his heart. She said there weren't any signs of HCM and it appeared to be an

ASD—or atrialseptal defect, an unrelated heart defect. I slowly shook my head, taking in the information she was giving, taking notes—more coronary terms to become familiar with. She went on to explain, "He was born this way. This is a fairly routine thing to fix surgically. You guys are really lucky that you found out about it now since he is asymptomatic and it could eventually be dangerous. You can schedule the TEE at the front desk. They'll tell you how to prepare for it. See you then."

Everyone left the room. As soon as the door closed, Emmanuel heaved a shuddering sigh. I handed him his shirt. "Wow," I said, too stunned to say much more.

⌁

In the next few days, living with the fact that Emmanuel had a heart at risk took me into a reverie of incidents in his life. Danger and grace: My first time in a hospital, besides being born, was when I was at term with him. I was an advocate for homebirth and had everything in place for one, but my water broke without labor starting. After waiting for the safe amount of time for contractions to start on their own, my midwife sent me to the hospital to be induced. I wept on the way there through the dark winding roads of the Berkshire night. A pitocin-induced labor in a place oriented to illness was counter to the dignity of natural childbirth that I had witnessed and experienced. I stopped crying and in a deep stillness began to pray. I visualized the membrane sealing up, that jellyfish-like translucence healing without a tatter.

At first the doctor on duty had been so impressed by my account of what happened that he asked if I was a nurse myself or in medical school. But when no trace of amniotic fluid was found with the "fern test," he brushed aside my experience as "probably just a bladder infection." I was sent home. Elizabeth, my midwife believed me. She had heard of fluke incidents where the amniotic sac had leaked and sealed on its own. The tissue was intact. Knowing full well the difference between where pee originated and amniotic fluid gushed from, I took my temperature every four hours, resigned to inducing labor if a fever indicated infection. Trusting that this baby would come at the right time, I held out for a spontaneous onset, which I anticipated at any moment. I rested in a succession of days set apart from ordinary time. For the first time in the pregnancy, I realized that this was a boy, and his name came strongly.

He came strongly too, after ten days of eager expectancy—on the verge of the autumnal equinox. When labor finally did start, it was sudden and dramatic. Before Elizabeth could make it, I had an uncontrollable urge to push. As soon as I surrendered to the fact that the birth was happening, I crouched down and joined the birth forces galvanized in my body, issuing instructions to his father as I did so. I pushed and a dark head crowned, then I panted to let a bluish creamy body emerge, slipping into my hands. I took the wet curled creature and raised him to my heart, where his dad placed a blanket over him. I suctioned him. He gave a good strong "Wah!" and looked directly in my eyes. I welcomed him in joy and relief: "Noah Emmanuel!" Gazing intently, he began to speak in garbled declarations, intent and determined to give expression. I had attended a score of births and never witnessed this quality of infant oratory. Elizabeth arrived by the time the placenta was ready to be delivered.

Danger and grace: years later, his piercing scream from afar slicing through me, I rushed to find him holding up his hand with a board attached to it and a large nail sticking through. Somehow I managed to wrench it out and get him to the doctor before panic hit. Somehow he managed to not suffer any nerve damage from the path the nail had taken through his palm. He was fortunate, they said. It healed completely, this stigmata at six.

Danger and grace: a few years later, at age nine, he had been hit by a car. I had insisted on accompanying him in the ambulance to the hospital. After they found no broken bones—only contusions and scrapes—a policeman went over the accident report with me. He had compiled the account from a number of witnesses who had seen Emmanuel being hit by a speeding motorist at the pedestrian crossing. He calmly told me that my son had been thrown thirty feet. Thirty feet? They had measured it. I had arrived to find Emmanuel lying on hard asphalt with paramedics all around him. I had no idea he had landed there from such a distance. After I signed the report, I tried to imagine how fast the car was going to be so forceful, and I sensed an angel muffling Emmanuel's fall—his resilience in bouncing. After he was better, Emmanuel told me he had learned something from the accident. I expected him to say something like "to look three times before crossing," but instead he declared, "I found out people love me."

⌐⌐

A few days after the first echo, we returned to the hospital for the more extensive test with Dr. H and a crew of technicians. From a new angle, I watched the cartography of his heart while he lay in a stupor. A thorough investigation revealed that the color-coded whoosh of blood was not going on its proper route. I was shown a close-up of the hole in his atrium—measured to be 1.16 cm. But that wasn't all: there were anomalous pulmonary veins.

While Emmanuel was in recovery, Dr. H made out a sketch for me, mapping out his deviant anatomy, its mis-directions. In concerned and compassionate tones, she explained that the ASD, in his case, had a twist: sinus stenosis. Basically, there were veins in the wrong place, taking oxygenated blood from his lungs back into the right atrium of his heart, which is normally where the unoxy-genated blood flows en route to the lungs. She took time explain-ing the complications that could arise from this: continued en-largement of his right atrium due to strain, or lung complications such as pulmonary hypertension. But the most common outcome from this condition, which usually went unchecked because of being asymptomatic, were severe and often deadly strokes, usually striking in the late twenties to early thirties. She was quick to point out that it has nothing to do with me.

She emphasized how fortunate it was to find this out now, so that we could intervene and prevent that. She told me how having a friend of hers die from this undiagnosed condition had led her into cardiology. Then she spoke of surgical repair, that it would need to be open heart surgery, not the patch procedure that I had already heard about—that was for less complicated ASD's. I was opposed to surgery, hoping that if I did enough research, I would find an alternative.

Was there one?

~

The question now was: How necessary was surgery? How high were the risks of leaving this condition alone? Were there any cases of spontaneous healing? Was this a structural problem that therefore has to be fixed in a structural way? I was thankful for my own experience as a heart patient to have a grasp of the anatomy, a recognition of the terms. I contacted doctor friends who were experienced in medical perspectives and more perceptive in this realm. I sought out expertise in congenital heart defects. I borrowed medical books and did research online. We got a second opinion from a surgically conservative cardiologist who affirmed that in this case it was absolutely necessary to repair it, the only safe thing to do. The more inevitable surgery appeared, the more I prayed like mad for some intervention.

There is a story of a mother who is wild with grief over the death of her child. The Buddha tells her to go find a house where death had not been known. She knocks on every door in her village—in each, she finds someone has lost a relative. I wasn't knocking on doors, but often when I brought up the decision I was facing, it seemed as if every fourth person or so had someone close to them who had undergone open heart surgery. A good friend's brother had an ASD with surgery at fourteen; a professor's wife had recently been operated on for another heart defect. My dear friend from England, Sarida, put me in touch with her friend who had one of the first open-heart surgeries in the 1950s by Lord Brock. Hearing these stories, where surgery was esteemed as a positive intervention, my resistance and fear began to lessen. Despite my focus on non-mechanistic views of the heart, I began to scrutinize when a mechanistic view could in fact be a gift.

I took to pondering destiny and how if we looked at restructuring Emmanuel's heart as a preventative measure, it could become an opportunity to alter an outcome. In earlier times without the diagnostic tool of an echocardiogram, this defect would not be noticed until it would be too late. If we waited for symptoms to develop, significant damage could be done—scary stuff: blood clots, heart failure, stroke, lung damage.

That summer, as I was coming to terms with Emmanuel's heart, a friend from long ago suddenly got in touch with me. Betsy and I hadn't seen each other for twenty-six years. I had spent five summers in Maine as a camper and then as a counselor-in-training of the artsy camp where she had been the co-director. She was a steady and guiding presence for me in the tumultuous years of my adolescence. I had swooned over her brother Joey from a distance. Summer after summer I spent in contemplation of his da Vinci-like beauty. Just lately I had noticed a resemblance of that stunning look in Emmanuel, a shared spark and humor. I was aware that Emmanuel was close to the age that Joey had been when I had met him.

Before I asked how Joey was, Betsy brought it up. Eighteen years ago, with absolutely no warning, he died of a massive stroke. He had been thirty. His autopsy revealed a rare congenital condition. This conversation stayed with me and served to make my son's risk far less abstract. The percentages ceased being anonymous and wore Joey's face, his glance merging into Emmanuel's. Surgery as intervention took on a heightened significance.

∼

After some hunting, I found the most qualified surgeon in Seattle for ASD and anomalous vein problems. His track record was good and his head nurse was willing to go over things with me, which was more than some. Once we found his office on a high floor of Swedish Medical, we filled out a number of forms and sat for a long spell with the posh waiting room entirely to ourselves. Eventually, a perky nurse led us back to an examination room and checked Emmanuel's vital signs. Pulse, blood pressure, weight. Finally, Dr. R came in. He was in his fifties, with gentle, deep-set dark eyes and strong hands. He was in a sky blue surgical gown, and I noticed rubber over his shoes. So they won't get bloody, I thought. He cuts people open.

After shaking our hands and introducing himself, he said, "I am sorry for the delay, but I needed to review the echocardiogram from Dr. H. Are you aware of what a large hole there is?" Neither Emmanuel nor I said anything. He held up his fingers to show, "It is quite significant: two and a half centimeters."

He went over how Emmanuel had a rarer form of ASD because of the reverse pulmonary veins. He assured us that it was a fairly straightforward procedure to add a little tube to his out-of-place veins and extend them through his septal hole to the other side. He had done it many times. Of course there are always risks in surgery, but Swedish Hospital was a state-of-the-art facility, and so on. I went through my list of questions and he answered them patiently and respectfully. He specialized in ASD's. He had lost count of how many heart surgeries he had performed, had been doing them three or four times a week for thirty years. Thousands by now. He gave me figures that I didn't retain: success rates, risks.

Emmanuel mostly wanted to know about timing. "I'm planning to go to England for a month after I graduate. I am hoping that we can just do the operation when I come back."

"That should be fine. As long as we handle this in the next few months it shouldn't be a problem. People can live with this condition and be fine. I just operated on a woman who didn't discover that she had it until she was seventy-five. She was doing fine until then. She was lucky." Then he went into the more common, less fortunate scenarios of stroke and such.

Emmanuel slowly nodded his head, chin leading, taking this in. A kind of hip way of saying "I get it." Dr. R shook our hands in turn and led us to his head nurse to schedule the operation.

At the end of July, Emmanuel returned to Seattle from his visit to England, a month before his heart surgery was slated. It was time to start the drawing of his blood on a weekly basis to build up a supply to have on hand during surgery. Autologous donation. Stepping into the medical realm of the blood bank, with its nurses, release forms and sterility made the reality of his becoming a patient much more vivid. I knew I had to reconcile myself to this intervention. I knew if I was to be any support at all to Emmanuel, I needed to let go of my resistance so my attitude wouldn't spill over.

I arranged to take off for a few days to stay up at the Marsh House on Whidbey Island, where I had led the fateful Council of All Beings seven summers before. By day I walked in the forest and along the beach. It was a novelty to be alone. Though I had left my children before a few times to attend programs, this was the first time I had been in solitude for many years. These few days to myself allowed my resistance and fears to melt away. In the imminence of surgery, all else seemed to fall away, superfluous. I have rarely been so focused in my life. I had wholly accepted that a radical restructuring needed to take place in Emmanuel's heart and that this would extend his life. Yes, this required an invasive act, but one that I now understood was necessary.

I returned to Seattle ready to be fully at Emmanuel's side. I was impressed by his attitude. After his initial anger, he had resigned himself to his heart defect and never doubted the operation. The morning for his surgery came. No breakfast. I gave him a high-potency homeopathic remedy to lessen the trauma. We went out into the chill of pre-dawn, he took a deep breath and said, "Let's get on with this." And so we did.

We had arranged for the operation to take place while his dad, Atum, was in town, because he wanted to be there. We picked Atum up at his apartment and I drove through the strangeness of empty downtown streets to the hospital. Emmanuel's admission procedures were scheduled for 5:30 a.m. We had already done the paperwork so now it was a matter of surgery prep. Overly-cheery nurses orchestrated his transition to patient. He changed into a gown and then we were asked to leave while he was shaven. Unexpectedly, instead of just his chest, the orderly ended up doing a full body shave. It turns out that this was routine for a coronary bypass, because it entails extracting a vein from the leg, but in this case, unnecessary. It appeared at the time to be some strange ritual of humiliation, an act of exposure.

Next, we went to meet the anesthesiologist, Dr. K and his assistants, whom he introduced as his team. Emmanuel was given a place on a rolling bed, curtained off from others awaiting narcosis as well. We could overhear various conversations going on: a discussion of the latest baseball scores; a daughter reassuring her elderly mother; a nurse making small talk with an elderly gentleman. Emmanuel's youth seemed incongruent with this place. They gave him a tranquilizer and, each in our own way, we wished him well. Then he began to fade and they wheeled him away to be put entirely under.

When the surgery began, I left Atum in the waiting room and went to the hospital chapel that I had scoped out at our pre-op visit. It was a small room with a few rows of chairs and a non-denominational altar with an eternal flame hanging above it. There was a recording of ocean sounds playing—the whoosh of waves sounding in the empty room. I took up my vigil, alone and not alone.

At some point, Atum came to give me the message that the anesthesiologist had called to say that they were about halfway through, and all was going well. After an hour, I returned to the lobby to be ready for the call from Dr. R. I prefer not to remember the images of Emmanuel's openness that besieged me at the time. The call came and I went to the desk to take it. "Hello, Dr. R here. No surprises. Emmanuel is doing fine. We've just finished the surgery and he is stabilizing. Everything went well. We did find that he had an extra pulmonary vein in the wrong place, so two-thirds of his blood volume was draining in the wrong side of the heart. That's all taken care of now. You can come up and wait to see him when he is ready in the ICU. I will meet you up there later."

In a room filled with the hum and display of life support and monitoring, Emmanuel groggily opened his eyes. I read at once the disorientation in his gaze. Atum and I both spoke to him in assuring tones. "We're here in recovery at the hospital. Everything is okay, the surgery went really well." I could see him take in the fact that he was unable to talk and that his arms were strapped down. "Remember, you are on the respirator until you are ready to breath on your own. It will be a little longer and then they'll take that out of your mouth and you can talk." He was struggling to indicate something. Gesturing as best he could with his hands tied down, he pointed in a thwarted way towards his face. Then began the effort to guess what he was trying to communicate. He grew more and more perturbed. That helplessness only lasted a couple of minutes at the most, but it was immense to me. We finally figured out that he wanted his face to be scratched, between his eyebrows.

I soon found that it was essential to be there with him in the hospital over the days and nights of his stay. I couldn't imagine being elsewhere. I was amazed at how much commotion was involved in a hospital stay, the amount of interruptions. There was a constant rotation of nurses, mostly fine but one truly "scary" one whom I had to hold to task. I discovered a fierce protectress in me, a mama lion. On the first night, he went into severely painful muscle spasms and semi-convulsions and no one knew what was going on and the pain meds didn't touch it. Finally Benadryl knocked him out and he slept. For some reason that didn't get noted in his chart and the next day when it happened again (when they woke him up for monitoring), there was all this fumbling about trying to figure out (again) what would help. Luckily, I was there to say, "Benadryl works!" I also demanded that, after that second ordeal of spasming, he be allowed to sleep uninterrupted through the night. I insisted that the top doc on the floor authorize that Emmanuel be left alone during the vital checks at three in the morning. With no intrusions, I discovered an undertone behind the high-tech efficiency, the presence of angels, pervasive peace in an unexpected place.

On the fourth day, Emmanuel was discharged, along with a slew of directions for his nursing care and recuperation at home. Precautions, warning signs, exercises, not to mention his "old lady socks" which he had to wear for what seemed like ages to reduce swelling. I set a room up for him on the ground floor until he could do the stairs. I tended to him there. Week by week, he improved.

On the fourth day, Emmanuel was discharged, along with a

After a month had passed, it was time to see Dr. R for a post-op appointment. We waited again in the same small room we had met him in, on the other side of surgery. He came in and examined Emmanuel, asked him questions, went over charts, "Everything is fine and you should continue to improve. If anything comes up, just call." He rose to leave, but I intercepted.

"Wait a minute. I just wanted to go over what you found during the operation." He had mentioned the extra vein, and I wanted to know more. Dr. R averted his eyes and said, "Okay. Just a moment." Then he left the room.

In a moment he was back. He took a seat, took a deep breath, and said, "Well, the interesting thing is …" he paused, " … once we got in there, we found that there wasn't actually any hole." I remembered the call from Dr. R in the OR. No surprises?

Later I looked at the surgical report. In the post-operative diagnosis, ASD appears in an unexpected way:

OPERATION:
1. Creation of Atrial Septal Defect
2. Patch repair of partial anomalous pulmonary
   venous return

In other words, when they opened Emmanuel's heart, there was no Atrial Septal Defect, "ASD"—the supposed hole between the chambers, after all. As a result, the first order of surgery ended up being to create a hole in his septum in order to correct the pulmonary return. Of course, the rerouting of his veins was needed, but I couldn't help imagining if they had opened him only to patch the supposed hole (the "ASD"). What of the bubbles we "saw" passing through from side to side, where they shouldn't be? The tissue was intact. Another strike against trusting medical imaging tests!

∽

*May, 2002*
*Seattle*

## Providential

*Is his heart okay?* I've just taken Kyrian, sixteen years old now, for a recommended heart screening to see if he is at risk. Driving home, I offer to stop for lunch and he suggests that we eat at Araya's, the Thai restaurant near his school. "Mom, you'll really like it," he says as we walk in. After heaping noodles and vegetables from the lunch buffet on our plates, we plunk them down at a table in front of a shrine. A full-bellied Buddha is surrounded by feminine deities, Quan Yins. Fat candles and sticks of incense remain unlit beside fruit offerings. There are replicas of lotuses, some budding and others in full bloom. We sit, facing one another. I gaze at a cascade of colorful figurines of the goddess of compassion, ornate and delicate, behind my son. A large sculpted frog crouches at their feet.

Like these goddesses, I am mostly background to Kyrian these days, busy as he is with work and school and friends. I bore him. The most I see of him is as a passenger in my humble Toyota. Mostly, he doesn't have much to say to me and answers my questions with terse replies. But lately, he's taken to using our time in transit to play tapes for me, mostly from the hip-hop record store where he's apprenticing to learn the business. He always tells me a bit about the artist, and the form, widening my acoustical horizons. Today, he introduced me to Saul Williams, his rhythmic voice pulsating with passion and poetry. I catch a line about how the heart is the philospher's stone.

In a year, I will highlight Williams' work in high school poetry courses I teach. In a couple of years, Kyrian will accompany this artist of the spoken word on stage, as a beat-boxer. But now Kyrian is just beginning to train his voice in the thrumming of vocal percussion evocative of the Tuvan throat singers of Mongolia.

Kyrian and I have been together more than usual this week: many hours yesterday, mostly waiting, for what turned out to be only a preliminary cardiology visit, and then today's echocardiogram ordered as a result of that drawn-out consultation. Since his brothers have cardiac abnormalities, he has tolerated these excursions, knowing we need to know: *Is his heart okay* ... or? ... Well, we'll cross that bridge when we come to it. A crossing I pray we won't have to make.

Meanwhile, we're resigned to the burden of suspense, until we know: *Is his heart okay?* Meanwhile, the phad thai has a delicious tang of fresh cilantro and ginger. I've brought lilies of the valley in with me and put them in my drinking glass so they don't wilt too much. This cluster was given to me by a "Sister of Providence" who works as the receptionist at the hospital where we just had Kyrian's test done. Devoted to "Our Mother of Sorrows," she wore a modified habit—hair tucked away in a shoulder-length veil, a gray dress that served as backdrop to the white crucifix on her matronly bosom. While I wondered, *Is his heart okay?* and Kyrian stared at the floor in tense silence, she made conversation with me: small talk about the upcoming merger of Providence Hospital (the first in Seattle) being taken over by the giant administration of Swedish Medical Center. I hope there will still be a place for her administrations, for ministry in medicine alongside the business of it.

After listening to the beats and booms of Kyrian's heart, amplified, after viewing transductions of his heart on the screen, this sister had awaited us in the reception area. As we left, she pressed the bouquet into my hand saying, "Here, these are for you, take them," as if she were an old friend, as if she were saying, "Don't worry ... have faith." That stream of tenderness stays with me, her simplicity a contrast to the extravagant shrine behind my son, who is now eating with gusto.

Over the next few days I do worry, waiting and wondering. Now that Kyrian's heart has been peered into, someone knows the results: *Is his heart okay?* Finally, I receive the definitive phone call from the cardiologist on my answering machine. I sit to brace myself, and reach out to touch the fading lilies of the valley, their scent still exuding. The doctor wanted to let me know the good news right away, "Your son's heart is perfect, no deviations are apparent at this time." A message I will keep and listen to again.

With a whoop of joy, I run downstairs to tell Kyrian. In his subterranean den, he is practicing his beat-boxing. The sonorous beat resounds in low boom and drone. His voice as deep as a bull-frog's; his throat a human thundering drum. He beats and booms. The primal rhythm of his faultless heart reverberates through the house.

～∽

*September, 2003*
*Seattle*

## Echoes

My thirteen-year-old daughter Rose and I are driving to the hospital. The day is bright with September sun, a day like any other in this Indian summer. I am hoping it stays that way, unremarkable. I'm not talking weather: we are on our way for Rose's heart to be screened. Along the way, she tells me that yesterday as she walked down the street, she found an intricate heart drawn in colored chalk on the pavement. "It was amazing!" She exclaims, "Not this kind…" as easily as a letter she traced the curve/point/curve so familiar in signifying heart, "but a real human one." I picture the four-fold chambers, septum, aorta. What lesson was this drawn for, not on a chalkboard, but on rough ground? A heart revealed on concrete, not necessarily anatomically correct, but close. I wonder if passersby will stop to look at it before the inflow of blue and outflow of red blur together and wash away when the rains come.

We park underground and make our way through the pedestrian tunnel with piped-in birdsong to the escalators that lead to the UW hospital. As we ascend I say, "Let's see, how many times have you been to a hospital?" Ahead of me, she turns to answer, "The one in Ballard for Marcia's ankle, Northwest to see Jeff's dad,

downtown when Taylor hit his head." More than I remembered.
"... and don't forget: Swedish." That is the hospital where Emmanuel had open-heart surgery. "Yes," I say. Yes. It seems like yesterday that I took him for the same test she is having today.

The ghosts of diagnosis accompany us. Echoes of others:
mine and her brothers, attesting to her genetic susceptibility.

We enter the hospital. It is teeming with people. I point
right, toward the elevators we need, and we make our way single
file in that direction. Mixed in with those of us with street clothes
are patients in hospital gowns: some in wheelchairs with IVs or
oxygen, some walking shakily with a cane or walkers. One woman
leans on another's arm for support, a mother and daughter by the
looks of it—similar eyes shine in wrinkled and smooth versions of
the same face. I look behind to make sure Rose is still there. It's
times like these, or crossing a busy street, that I still have to hold
back from instinctively reaching out to hold her hand. She is close
behind. We pass a crowded side lobby, catch a glimpse of a woman
with a bruised face and swollen surgical wounds, unbandaged. We
hurry on.

On the fourth floor, we step out of the elevator to the cardiac
clinics. Outside the echocardiogram lab, there is a bronze plaque
of a heart on the wall. Tilted, its four chambers evident, the hollow
aorta thrusting out.

"Hey, this is like the drawing I saw yesterday!" She exclaims
and we move closer to investigate.

"Pretty neat, isn't it? Soon we'll be looking at yours."

I've been emphasizing the wonder of this upcoming test:
to see a heart in motion. How the pictures are created by sound
waves bouncing off the heart structure itself. How it looks like a

pulsating flower, beautiful to see in motion. I've asked Rose to consider how da Vinci would react to see a live heart pulsating so. I know she is anxious about her heart. She is not the only one. Originally prescribed for children at risk when they are full grown, this diagnostic echocardiogram is now recommended at puberty. Rose has requested recently to get the test over with—to know one way or another.

One way or another, we will know before long.

I have been here before, waiting. The pastel interiors of this waiting room blurs together with others: Zenith cardiology, Seattle; The Multi-Specialty Clinic, Olympia; NIH, Maryland; St. James, London; Swedish Hospital, Seattle. I am suspended, surrounded by homogenous chairs and coffee tables stacked with magazines; waiting as patient; waiting as mother. I'd give anything to have it stop with me. It seemed the worst part of the disease was the possibility of leaving my children motherless before they grew up, but then I learned that it was hereditary. I look across at my last child to be screened. She has just recently reached my height and will no doubt join her brothers in towering over me soon. Her dark brown hair streams down over her shoulders. Her deep brown eyes are accented by darkened lashes and eyeliner, adding a touch of Goth that can't subdue her bright inquisitiveness.

I want a drink of water but there is only a cooler devoid of its usual plastic urn, a stack of empty bottles beside it. I can almost hear their emptiness. No water. A young man in blue scrubs comes into the room. "Rosemary?" he asks.

"Yes." We rise, a bit surprised at her formal name.

"I'm Alan. I'll be performing your echo today. Right this way." We turn right and start walking down the hall. "So you're mom?"

"Indeed," I nod.

"With the HCM?" He doesn't leave me time to answer. "One of many myopathies in the family, right?"

"Yeah, well, two out of three of her siblings have heart defects." I'm hoping for symmetry here: two out of four.

We enter the dimly-lit lab filled with the low hum of the echocardiogram machine. A glorified computer, it takes up a major portion of the small room: black wires coiled up in front of the blank monitor, just beside the huge keyboard/control panel. There is a bed beside it. He gives Rose a gown. "Strip from the waist up and leave it open in the back." He opens the door to a changing room for her. Alan looks over the forms and recognizes Dr. Stout as the cardiologist, putting in a good word about her work at Children's Hospital. He explains to me that the results will go to her. I tell him that it is difficult to do the test and have to wait for the results, considering the presence of heart abnormalities in the family. He responds by saying he would feel the same way and offers to page Dr. Stout. Rose has joined us in her hospital gown. Alan points to the bed. "Have a seat," he says, as he leaves the room.

"How're you doing?" I ask Rose. Robed in light blue, with her graffitied jeans sticking out below, she is poised on the bed, a delicate hand palm down on each knee.

"Fine," she replies. I nod my head, appreciating her brave determination. As a child she was terrified of doctors, ever since she had a long cotton swab stuck up her nose when she was three. For years, she clung to me whenever we encountered anything remotely medical. It's only been a couple of years since assurance took the place of that fear.

Alan returns. "Okay, let's start." He has Rose lie on her side.

I settle into a seat a few feet from the screen. He tells Rose about the electrodes he is putting on her, about how the pictures will be cross-sections of the heart; about the goop that will be cold in order to allow a good reading. The lights go off and an image appears on the screen. "So the way it works is the sound has to carry through water—in this case, blood. This black here is the blood. He points in a hurried cross. "Left ventricle; right ventricle; lower; upper." Lying with a good view of the screen, Rose's dark brows are slightly drawn in concentration. Her quizzical look probes this black and white abstraction. Soon the *whoosh* of her heartbeat joins the movement on the screen. I notice that the numbers beside her heart rate per minute vary: 74. 84. 76. I watch the clapping motion of the mitral valve, open/close/open/close. Too early to know if it's celebratory applause.

This screen, bordered with the squiggle of heart waves, fuses with so many others: the one that showed that Chris had indications of the same abnormality that I had had. It becomes the one I watched of Emmanuel's heart. The moment I knew something was wrong by the subtle signs of the technician's concern: the way he kept repeating the hemodynamic readings and started asking questions. How I began to waver then, my own heart quickening in alarm—the closing in of dread. That same shakiness tugs at me again.

I look away from the screen, stare at the machine itself: "ACUSON" in bold letters of teal along the frame. A high-tech evolution of auscultation, the hands-on precursor of this diagnostic tool, ascertaining heart size by tapping one's bent fingers and listening for reverberations. Because of widespread reliance on "Acuson" and the like, medical researchers are seeing a decrease in auscultation skills in doctors, and less confidence in using that form of direct listening.

Still trying to steady myself, I squeeze my hands together, reminding myself that the heart of her third brother, Kyrian, was fine, just fine. Hypervigilant, I watch to see if anything Alan does will reveal a sign of danger as the test proceeds. Her heart rate is still fluctuating: 88. 76. 80. I don't know what is normal anymore. I notice the different views are called sweeps. The sound waves are sweeping her aorta and its threefold valve now. Alan's voice almost startles me. "Here's the tricuspid valve." Or is it a seaflower, pulsing with waves?

"Isn't that beautiful?" I ask Rose.

"Yeah."

Another sweep, from below, reveals all four chambers. Dancing.

"This view always reminds me of a bell pepper," I say.

I see her narrow her eyes a bit, "Yeah … " says Rose

"You mean when it's sliced open? I can see that," says Alan.

"Yes, a cross section. It has a similar structure."

"You should see what some of our patients on medication see when they take this test! Wild stuff."

Rose and I both laugh, polite and shallow.

After a few moments of pressing keys, Alan asks me, "Do you have obstruction with your condition?"

I pause, remembering the onset of symptoms: words I stumbled over at first come back to me, left ventricle obstruction with severe regurgitation a part of my original diagnosis.

"There is actually a question if I have the disease in the first place. There has been an ongoing debate about it between the top HCM researcher at NIH and his counterpart in the UK."

"Well, they can do some tap dancing about semantics, but obstruction is obstruction. You either have it or you don't. It would show."

I debate if I should share the dispute over angles and inter-pretations, and feel weary at the prospect. "My first echoes showed obstruction, but then later ones showed none. It's a long story." I sigh, slightly. He nods slowly, a clenched jaw leading. If he wasn't being polite, I am sure he would be shaking his head instead. I am hoping that he's not thinking obstruction from something he's seen and can't say.

A few moments later Alan is paged and excuses himself as he steps out of the room. No sweeps on the paused screen, Rose, still wired up, wiggles her toes. Her hair on the pillow is a storm around her. Her full lips are slightly parted, relaxed. Her eyes are keen. "You're doing great, Rose," I say, and I mean it.

Alan returns.

Standing, smiling, he tells me, "That was a call from Dr. Stout. These days, because of lawsuits and such, we are not free to talk about these things with the patients. But I went over the basic results so far and we agreed that it would be okay to tell you: this echo is nothing to lose sleep over."

I pause, inwardly repeating his words, which have come a long distance to reach me. I can't quite believe that he said this, but he did. Nothing to lose sleep over. "That is really good to hear." My hands loosen their grip. "Thank you!"

He deliberately stresses his next words slowly, "Yes, she won't be needing another of these for a long time."

Rose and I look at each other. Her eyes are bright. We are both smiling. Maybe this means ... could it be ... are we allowed to dare to ... nothing to lose sleep over ... my baby is alright. Her life ahead will not be overshadowed by a heart defect.

Alan is saying, "Just one last view now. Please lie flat on your back."

He places the probe just beneath Rose's collar bone, beaming downwards into her rib cage. This angle reveals an arching I don't recall, "I haven't seen that before." Then I laugh at the obvious, "But how could I have, from that position."

Alan joins my laughter, "Not very well! This is the aortic arch from above."

"Aortic arch," I repeat,

" ... where the oxygenated blood flows back into the body."

Rose's eyebrows soften as she watches, almost dreamily. I look back to this bend of the heart, where the blood flows red, renewed. It is new to me: this graceful vault, this cathedral curve: a renewal, a covenant: its perfect arc.

⤫

## Universal Heart

I celebrate you, polyvalent universal heart:

I honor you as the ray of Bhakti: hands to
work and hearts continually praising, be it
Nataraj,
cosmic dancer, or blue-skinned Krishna,
multifold lover, each gopi infused with his
fluted song; or devoted Hanuman with his
chest held open to reveal his lord and queen
in heart cavern abiding, monkey-self
devoted to inner sovereignty
kept steady in song.

I honor you as the ray of bodhisattvas,
beings who
include absolute extinction of all creation's
suffering within enlightenment's terms, and
serve eternally in a jeweled fluid stream of
compassion, be it all seeing
Avalokitesvara, of the many arms
outreaching, or Tara who came forth from
his tear, present to all anguish, lotus heart
blooming in sludge, or the ruby padme
dakinis' transformation: passion to
equanimity.

I honor you as the ray of Zarathustra, with
heart of celestial earth, sensitized to the
archangelic bodies, entrusted to our care:

Armaiti, living earth, all gracious Anahita,
cleansing waters, flowing unimpeded;
Attar, purifying fires, burning fiercely
Vayu, vibrant air, all pervasive
Each one revered, sourced in the undying
creator spirit of the sun.

I honor you as the ray of Christos,
indwelling spirit celebrated through
communion; heart of Jesus encircled in
thorns, flaming; heart of Mary pierced
through with sword—tender woundings a
threshold for love to blaze through. Heart of
Francis with all creatures communing,
Mother Theresa serving the poorest of the
poor, each one: holy. Beyond orthodoxy, all
life made sacred through sacrifice.

I honor you as human will fulfilled through
surrender to all in awe, continual effacement in
a literacy of the unnamable: the ninety-
nine names of Allah, and the way those
qualities stream into creation, revealed
through Mohammed, peace be upon him,
whose chest was torn open by the divine
messenger, Gabriel, to remove all poison
from his heart, thus making him a prophet of
unity.

I honor all your many facets, universal heart.

*1978 – 1982 and onwards*
*Swarthmore, Pennsylvania*

## Planetary Heart

Our Universal Worship services were held in a room in the Sufi House with many glass doors. Above the altar, a span of windows framed a stained glass winged heart, inscribed with a crescent moon cradling a five-pointed star. Sunlight flooded through gemmed wings of sapphire and azure hues that dazzled into curls of feather. Ivory candles placed in crystal holders arced in a crescent around a higher light. Gold-covered scriptures were placed before each light: the Hindu Upanishads, Buddhist Sutras, the Zend Avesta of Zarathustra, the Torah, the Bible, the Qu'ran, and a small book of Sufi verses honoring the path of the heart. White-robed, I invoked the unity of spirit while kindling each candle from the central flame.

A luminous heart with outspread wings pervades Sufi mysticism. Not bird's wings, but the pinions of angels with dazzling plumes. I know it well. One of my devotions was to embroider an altar cloth with this symbol. Gold stitch by gold stitch with shimmering thread, I knotted feathers of the soaring heart into buttery silk.

Over the years, though, I grew to see my attraction to this heavenly heart as a form of evasion, as I began to counter this wingedness with an insignia of rooted hearts. Gradually, rather than searching the scriptures, I preferred divining Nature's script. Sermons morphed into stories, altar flames were replaced by candles kindled at mealtime grace and those at my children's bedside.

The altar I serve now honors a geology of depths. I praise our hearts, ever-questing, rooting down through fertile soil, rot and decay feeding new life, circulating through seasons; through wasteland; through Earth with its diastole and systole of ocean tides, veined through with rivers, with gems, pulsing with ores; to branch down through all strata to the fiery core. And this wisdom: that "Earth" and "Heart" are both contained in "Hearth." Let this be my hearth then: a planetary heart, winged yet rooted, seeped through with living waters, fire at the core.

❧

*Spring, 2004*
*Seattle*

## Towards Restoration

At the site of a former cranberry bog, a modern temple stands. Rites of consumerism take place here daily amidst acres of asphalt. Despite the abundance of shoppers, the southern parking lot— designated for overflow—is seldom used. Even obscured as it is in blacktop, one can read "stream bed" in the sloping ground. Listen—beneath the more obvious flow of traffic from the nearby interstate, the sound of rushing water: a creek source piped below where we stand. Here in the scorching wasteland of the parking lot there is a circular grate, a gateway of sorts. Iron bars criss-cross over the imprisoned water source. Subterranean waters gush and burble, a dark shimmering below us.

We have traced the creek to its origin. Annie, visiting from Forest Row, offers her sensitivity. Golden-maned, she tunes in to the subtle realms of elemental beings: unseen frequencies of life force. Francie, with her short-cropped hair cresting like some exotic bird, brings her devotion. A sculptor, she creates guardians, informed by sense of place, and dreams of making one to abide here to help free displaced water beings. I bear witness. Against the backdrop of heavy traffic, we stand in the stretch of barrenness above the water source. "I feel sadness," says Francie. Her simple words resonate. In the words of Joni Mitchell, this "paved paradise" is the cost of so-called progress.

"It feels as if Heaven and Earth have been divided here, not meeting as they would if the source were undisturbed," suggests Annie. The rift of disruption interferes on so many levels, measurable and immeasurable.

I recall the ancient stories, the etiology of wasteland mapped out in the loss of the voices of the springs, the loss of the nurturing of the wells once their guardians were assaulted. I think of Francie's sculptures gestating into the well-maidens that originally held golden cups and served wayfarers whatever nourishment they needed: how these diminished waters once flowed and provided sustenance; how this stream was home to salmon who returned here for eons until their way was obstructed—a corollary to the way of the maidens, whose cups were appropriated for other means.

The story that claims me in this place is "The Elucidation," a prequel to the Grail Quest.

*In ancient times, the country of Logres flourished, with wellsprings of purely flowing waters, each with its guardian maiden, who, with golden cups, offered sustenance to wayfarers. And so it was for generations until a king, Amangons, betrayed the peace and raped a well-maiden, and so set in motion the demise of the once-verdant kingdom. The king's men carried off the golden cups to serve the king. In response, the service of the wells ceased. The land once lush was laid to waste: trees lost their leaves, meadows withered and plants died. The wells dried up and so the way to the court of the Royal Fisherman—"he who made the land bright with his treasures"—was obscured, no longer accessible.*

*Eventually news of this reached the court of King Arthur and the Knights of the Table Round. Hearing of the devastation in the neighboring kingdom, the knights vowed to recover the wells and protect the maidens. But when they finally arrived in that desolate land, it was far too late. All the wells were dry and not a single well maiden was left. In the scrubby forests Arthur's men found heavily armed knights guarding women. They took one of these knights back with them to Arthur's court and there he told that they were bound to travel through this desolate land until the court of joy would be found to make the land bright again.*

*So the challenge of quest was set before the knights: to seek the court of the Fisher King, who was grievously wounded. Many sought but only a few found this otherworldly court, magnificent in splendor. There they witnessed the procession of the Grail Bearers, who, in the same manner as the original well-maidens, offered whatever sustenance was needed by the seeker. But time and again, no inquiry was made as to the wound that the Fisher King bore, and so the Grail Castle disappeared as if it were a dream, locked within another realm.*

*But eventually a seeker returned after a lifetime's journeying and he became the Grail Winner, known as "he who frees the waters." He asked the wounded king the simple, healing question, "What ails thee?" And all was redeemed. The waters flowed once again; fountains that had dried up ran into the meadows; fields*

*were green; the trees bore fruit; gardens prospered and forests flour-*
*ished. The court of joy was reclaimed once more in the world, no*
*longer separate.*

Here in acres of asphalt that surround the mall, I can't help
but notice the King's name: A-man-gone(s)—so telling of this
rupture from source. Man truly gone, cut off from any sense of
wellspring, caught up in the desolation of soul that perpetuates the
commerce taking place in this artifice, a far cry from the seasonal
villages native tribes-people created to harvest the cranberries that
once grew rampant here. But as appealing as the dream of return
might be, it is not an option, nor is finding the Fisher King in
some remote spirit world.

Still, the knights of the story are not as outdated as they may
appear. Forty years ago, when Northgate Mall was being built, per-
mits were issued to bury the creek "temporarily," and to this day
it remains hidden. In the last few years, a battle has raged between
Simon Brothers, the largest shopping mall corporation in the US,
which owns Northgate Mall, and local environmentally concerned
citizens. The Thornton Creek Legal Defense Fund (TCLDF) was
founded in 1999 to counter the proposed redevelopment project
that sought to double the size of the shopping center and entomb
Thornton creek in a 2,200 foot long culvert, covering it with parking garages, mega-apartment residences and a multiplex cinema.
In a hearing that year about the lack of an environmental impact
statement, the examiner determined that, "When the creek was
put into a culvert, it ceased to exist ..." extrapolating that therefore it had no need to be protected or restored.

Luckily, in July 2000, that ruling was appealed and Simon
Brothers was ordered to work with the creek activists and take

into consideration the necessity of daylighting the creek. Thus a legal precedent was set to protect urban stream health and salmon habitat restoration. A few months later, Simon Brothers put the property up for sale. Years passed and a more sympathetic mayor and developer became part of the equation. Just recently, a plan has been approved by the Seattle City Council that is a compromise for both sides. It includes a decrease in building volume with landscaping around the creek running through. At the same time, pipes will run underneath for storm overflow.

No ground broken yet, we walk over the abandoned lot and cross the street and down to a wooded area where the stream emerges from the culvert. When I see the waters set free, in witnessing their meander in this riparian corridor, I feel joy. This area was restored a few years ago by Earthcorps, a group of youth from the world over. This was a project for their annual gathering here in Seattle to learn about restoration. The area has grown a bit wild now, with a sign indicating volunteer work parties to come. Three grand willows crown the area, morning glories twining about their swaying branches. I have often seen them from my car in passing and am pleased to make their acquaintance closer up.

Images and associations cascade through me as strongly as the voice of waters beside us. Wasteland, wounding, wounded maidens; the way of dominating kings against women and waters; the insatiability of materialism that blinds and binds us so. But despair fully acknowledged becomes poignancy, which opens the ability to be present to this vibrant beauty, this stroke of wildness only a stone's throw away from prime wasteland. A glimmer of hope awakens. The Grail is not transcendent; it is transformative. The "Court of Joy" is not afar; indeed another translation for it is "body."

Here in our bodies, in our lives, the oppression of well-maidens dwells. Yet we will sing again, serving the waters. Here in our bodies, in our lives, the Fisher King is sustained in woundedness, awaiting the question that heals simply by acknowledging injury. Here in our bodies, in our lives, the quest for reclamation takes place: to be reclaimed to wholeness and holiness in the Court of Joy—our own bodies fully present, aware of our embeddedness within the living cosmic Earth.

Annie, Francie, and I walk back across black macadam and return to the creek source. We stand around the grate and hold hands in silence. Taking turns, we each say a prayer to invite spirit back into the body of these waters that gurgle below us. Through our intention, we become the bridge, singing out and sounding. As our voices find harmony and merge, I understand now that the locus of restoration is our hearts, streaming now in love and envisioning. Let the waters be free and the wasteland be transformed. Let the salmon one day return. Our voices merge and blend with the creek below us, waters that, however diminished, will be freed once again.

∽

*Fall, 2003*
*Seattle*

## Books of the Dead

The office of Lake View Cemetery is subdued as I look through the listings of the deceased, to find a beloved poet's grave among a multitude. I've walked around the graveyard already, searching to no avail, surprised by the throng of tombstones. The hushed but cheerful receptionist, Ms. Burns, looks on as I scan the pages. I glance up from the enormous volume, "There are so many graves here." I hazard a guess. "How many, a thousand?"

"Just over. We have a lot of people here."

Under "1996," I find: Levertol, Denise. "Here, this must be it—spelled wrong. "

Ms. Burns comes over. "So it is." She writes a heavy V over the L at the end of the listed name.

"She's my favorite poet," I tell her.

"I like her work too."

On the corner of a photocopy of a map she writes down the coordinates to locate the plot: Section 58 ½ 204B.

Then she highlights a little square in yellow. "It will be easy to find, not far from the road; you can drive right up."

I wouldn't think of making this pilgrimage in any other way than by foot. I walk back across the street. There is no pedestrian path through the grand gateway entrance, but there's no danger of traffic in this unfrequented place. The bright October day sparkles fresh after a long awaited rain. I enter and walk up the main road till it divides. I pause to check the plot map: left here, then bear around right, then left again.

I continue, uphill.

Amidst the granite rows, two men are digging a fresh plot with shovels, a backhoe parked beside them. No one else is in sight. I've driven by these iron-fenced acres countless times, knowing it as Denise Levertov's cemetery. I've pictured her interred on this highest point in our Emerald City, facing out eastward towards the lake and mountains—an open horizon.

Now, I take my last turn, up the slope, and I see it, in the shade of a towering tree: a tombstone like no other. Flanked by two unremarkable white-gray granite markers, a rectangle stands mid-rib high, entirely black. But somberness gives way to levity: perched upon it is a sculpture—unpolished white marble, mostly rounded with one slightly convex surface, dipping in. Egg-like, bird-like, yet substantial, it stands out the way her verse of "organic form" did amidst so many variations of conformity. On the ink-black surface of the dark metal square, her name and dates are engraved in familiar lettering—the same font as her poetry books. A final typeface on this ka'ba-like block.

Jeweled raindrops glisten in the branches just above my head. Atlas cedar. Silence gathers as I stand, beyond words, paying homage to her. How can I express my gratitude? I haven't brought flowers, and anyway, they'd wither.

I notice a fresh fall of cedar cones on the ground. How would she describe them?

The size of my thumb
but rounded, brown, hard-shelled—

I gather the cones and approach where her remains lie. Kneeling down, I arrange a crown just above where her head molders back to earth. It's grave here in the graveyard—and I am as well, in proximity to undercurrents of decay, bones, and ash. What remains? The flight of poems crafted by a hand that lies still now. Her voice become a currency outliving her speech.

I stand with wet knees, my living eyes busy taking in this shadow place on a dazzling day. The sun-wheel of cones rest in the rain-diamonded grass blades. No sheen on her iron-black grave. I lean back against the enormous trunk of the Atlas cedar, knowing it's tall enough so I can see it when I drive by, and that its roots emanate far below, concealed. Her words well up in the silence:

*O taste and see!*

I'll take it as a mandate, to drink my fill till doomstroke.

Ten years ago I discovered that it was common for people with my heart condition to drop dead with no warning. So acute the dance of death became, it spurred me to not take anything, anything, for granted. Seeing death just over my left shoulder, I entered into life more fully. A life that would be ending now if I had stayed on the medication prescribed for me then. I recently found out that by subduing the heart muscles, Lopressor thins the myocardium so much that it dwindles away: ten years maximum.

I have a few cedar cones from my beloved poet's guardian tree in my pocket as I go back down the hill. I will put them in the warmth of my study beside her books—volumes I began gathering thirty years ago. I know they will eventually open and release their papery seeds. Perhaps some will lodge in me. I will circulate her precious voice into the world. Close to exiting the cemetery, I notice new marble monuments, their unengraved faces shining blank, advertising final real estate. Not yet. For now, cherishing each breath, I walk clear from the loom of sudden expiration.

For now.

> *The books of the dead*
> *shake their leaves,*
> *word-seeds fly and*
> *lodge in the black earth.*[5]
> —Denise Levertov

*May, 2004*
*Seattle*

## Change of Course

I have been working hard all month, can't remember the last time I took a break. It's rare for me to go out in the evenings, except for my mother-chauffeur duty or faculty meetings, but it's Saturday night, Rose is busy, and I am ready to celebrate. I should go to the Eurythmy performance that some of my students and colleagues are involved in, but a new writer friend, Deborah, has invited me to her reading and I am ready for something out of the ordinary. There is a bounce in my step as I lock up the house and make my way to my car. The spring evening is full of promise. "Ready for adventure," I murmur to myself.

Deborah's reading is in West Seattle. I've plotted the way— south a ways, then west over the bridge, and then I'll have to follow my handwritten directions for a series of turns. I've allowed half an hour, time to get lost a bit in the unknown streets of that neighborhood over and across an inlet. I turn on to Aurora Avenue, the main road south through the city—moving very slowly now. I put on a tape and sing along with Phoebe Snow, "I want something real in my life, 'fore I die." A few moments later, the traffic is completely stuck. Is a traffic update available? But it's not rush hour and the radio with "Swing Years and Beyond" offers no help. Brake lights as far as I can see. Standstill. After fifteen minutes of inching along for only a few blocks, I decide to turn off and use the interstate. It will add on ten extra minutes or so, and I hate being late, but at least it will be moving.

But it's not. As I approach, I get a glimpse and see my alternate route is completely jammed. The reading starts in five minutes. A block ahead, on the left, the University Towers rises, the hotel where the dance performance I decided not to go to is being held. The next thing I know, I have parked the car and am in the lobby. I guess I am not going to see Deborah after all. Outside the ballroom doors, I stand in line to buy my ticket. A crowd assembles in the lobby with people I know from the high school where I teach and the larger community.

After recognizing each other across the room, a slender man with delicate features whom I've met once or twice comes up to me with his daughter. In a surprisingly warm greeting, we guess if we remember one another's names correctly. We do. It's David and Genevieve, who was my special charge for six weeks, four years ago when I worked as a first grade classroom assistant, before she left for a smaller class with a teacher who could meet her special needs. I can see she is still shy, as she half-hides behind her father, an electrician who worked in my house a couple of times. He smiles, his attention compels me to want to stay close by. It's been years since we met. When David asks what I've been up to, I tell him about being in graduate school and teaching. He tells me about being so sick he almost died this winter, after he and Genevieve's mom split. The quality of our sharing deepens. This is what will stay with me—his absolute honesty, openness. I hadn't realized how rare it is. Suddenly: no artifice.

Genevieve looks on, taking everything in with her probing brown eyes. When I speak to her, she responds by glancing away, no answer. I remember her snuggling up in my lap, day after day, sucking her thumb and clutching her blanket, burrowing into me if things got too loud. I am not sure she remembers me at all. The doors open and we go our separate ways, only to meet again inside. I settle down with some friends to watch scenes from The Magic Flute portrayed in Eurythmy—Papagano, a birdman in a riot of color, Tamino searching for his beloved and vows to free her from a villain, come what may. Sweet promises of the Queen of the Night if he succeeds.

At intermission, David is beside me again. I ask him if he knows where a water fountain is and he points out the way to a vending machine, downstairs. A few moments later, as I rise from getting a bottle of spring water, I feel a gentle touch on my elbow from behind. "I see you found the water." In that moment I have no inkling that over time, he will fulfill a deeper thirst that has left me wary of mirages. I am only aware at the end of the evening, when we encounter one another again in the lobby, that I want to tell him that I survived a serious illness; I want to say I'd like to talk more, sometime. But I have suddenly become as shy as Genevieve, who is peering out from behind his arm, which she holds tightly in front of her as a shield.

I leave, completely disarmed by David. At the end of the week, I wake up one morning with a clear impulse—a voice that I trust resounds in me, "Let David know: grace exists." As if my healing is a done deal. Set and stable. As if my heart condition is behind me for good. I want him to know that miracles are possible, that there is hope in his despair.

I track down his number. Summoning my courage, I call him and invite him to go for a walk, telling him that I'd like to talk more. A few days later, he picks me up. We haven't set where we'll walk. Before I suggest Golden Gardens, our nearby beach on the Sound, he asks if I'd like to go there. As we head that way, he tells me that he studies astrology and that he's just been to an inspiring conference. He asks me what my sun, moon and rising sign are. When I tell him, he looks directly in my eyes and says, "So you like a man who is assertive yet nurturing." Little do I know that these are the very qualities he will bring to me, later on.

✼

*July, 2004*
*Seattle*

## Cardiac Consultation XII: Middle Way

The morning sun shines through a glass prism that hangs in my eastern window, making a rainbow across my chest. Orange, yellow, and green blur in a wash of light with a faint line of blue on one edge, red on the other. Shining on me: the light of full spectrum, with the middle accentuated.

Today I will tread the middle way, between the previous extremes of diagnosis. On one end, a dire scenario and severe limitation; on the other, being told not to consider myself a heart patient at all. Slowly, over the past week or so, I've begun to come to terms with something being amiss with my heart again, after nine years with no symptoms whatsoever. I know that at forty-six, my body is in the turmoil of approaching menopause, and that heart palpitations are common among women going through "the change." But the turbulence in my heart has been too consistent to qualify for a common disturbance. Naive of me, considering my history, not to be in the care of a cardiologist, but that only shows how well I have felt. Until these latest symptoms, it's only occurred to me in passing. I always figured I'd deal with it if I had to. Now I have to. Now I will.

It began on a trip to drop Rose off at her horse camp in Goldendale, a couple of hundred miles southeast of Seattle. The low desert didn't agree with me. Despite the fact that my heart was pounding excessively fast, I kept calm as I slept, or tried to, in a room in the hexagonal lodge built around an open fire pit. Coyotes' howls filled the night. A tiger-striped kitten curled up right next to my racing heart, her purr a comfort. I left early to get back home and call a doctor. As I drove alone over the winding roads of the anticline Umtanum range, I became increasingly unsure if I would make it out of the scrublands. In fact, my pulse was so accelerated that I had moments of being downright terrified. I thought of hummingbirds, with their heart rate of 500 beats per minute. Clenched and praying as I drove, I made it back home to Seattle, and took my hummingbird heart back into the hands of cardiac specialists.

At the congenital heart disease clinic at the University of Washington Medical Center, I agreed to have an echocardiogram taken. Three sonographers pondered over the records that I brought from my thorough echo in England. The team included Alan, who had been so compassionate when he did Rose's echo and had told me in code that there were no problems with her heart. I noticed the replays and picked up on the concern. They spoke to one another of their trouble in getting the planes to agree. The bone-white-coated doctor who joined them for awhile, his whole body a scowl, turned to tell me, "Shop talk. Nothing to be scared of. The bottom line in cardiology is: if you feel okay, you are okay." But his job is all about revealing what is hidden in heart structure, regardless of whether it is experienced or not. When they talked amongst themselves in medical terms, thinking

I couldn't follow, I surprised them by joining in. When the doctor left, Alan, still trying to get measurements to agree, looked directly in my eyes and said, "This isn't easy." I nodded, accustomed to not fitting into usual cardiac parameters.

This morning, I consider how the planes in my echo didn't agree, at least at first, and wonder what is true. I take strength this morning from where the dazzle of rainbow lands—of all places: across my heart. But still, I am bracing myself for what I may hear.

I compose myself, caught between wanting to know what the facts are and wishing there was nothing to know. Amongst the three doctors that saw me last week, "Grace" and "Stout" are included in their names. I find an omen in this, knowing both of these qualities are required now.

In a cold gray room in the hospital, I wait alone. A "congenital fellow" (research intern) comes in and nervously greets me. Overly stiff for his early thirties, square-framed, clean-cut and blond, he clears his throat to tell me that the echo shows that I have an indisputable case of obstructive cardiomyopathy.

Dr. O, the cardiologist, enters the cold room, and I rise to greet her. In her early fifties, she is slender with red hair and freckles, an electric stethoscope around her neck. Her glasses are too big for her face. I've been told that she is preeminent in interpreting echocardiography, and lectures on this worldwide. Today she seems brisk yet subdued. After a firm handshake, we sit down, while the congenital fellow stands at attention, shaking his head when I offer the seat beside me. Dr. O's drab voice mirrors a lack of warmth as she gets down to the matter of fact: scenarios and treatments, now that it is established that I do have a substantial case of obstructive hypertrophy. Now that I have been re-sentenced.

"Of course you already know about the risk of sudden death ... "

She asks about my activity level. When I tell her that I walk a couple of miles a few times a week and that I sometimes get a tingling numb sensation down my left arm when I do, she tells me with a severe look, "Well, certainly don't do anything more active than that."

Dr. O goes over the range of treatments: septal reduction surgery (more precise now due to the use of echocardiography during open-heart surgery); septal ablation (killing off some of the cardiac muscles by inducing a controlled heart attack with alcohol); a defibrillator implant to take over if the heart goes into fatal arrhythmias (the newest procedure, still working out the kinks). When I ask about the use of pacemakers, so highly recommended to me at NIH, she dismisses them as having never panned out. We discuss the pros and cons of each scenario. Then she offers, "We'll start with medication. Since you didn't do well on the beta-blocker before, we'll try another class of drugs—a calcium channel inhibitor."

"Verapamil?" I ask. She nods while the congenital fellow, still standing in the corner, scrawls out a prescription. I look directly into Dr. O's brown eyes to tell her, "I'd like to hold off on medication. I want to watch my symptoms for a while and see how frequent they are and then decide. I've worked with alternative ... " I correct myself, " ... complementary therapies before, and they helped a lot, so I'll be doing that again."

She almost cuts me off to say they will give me the prescription anyway, "just in case." She asks about my children, saying all of them will need to be tracked, that HCM might not show up in the two who had clear echoes until they are in their twenties, that after all I was thirty-five when it presented. That of course they will need to watch me with an echo every year, "to see how it is progressing." It—this monstrous over-musculature of heart cells.

I ask if there might be a stethoscope so I can listen to my heart myself. She takes the black tubing from around her neck and hands me her high-tech instrument. As I put the ear pieces in my ears, she places the round sensor above my heart murmur and turns it on. I listen to my heart obstructed. *Ba-boom-whoosh. Ba-boom-whoosh.* My iambic churns, out of sync with any semblance of pentameter.

～

Downstairs, I ask for directions and make my way through to an adjoining building for a copy of my medical records: more to add to my file. Then I walk city blocks' worth of narrow hallways with low ceilings and polished tan vinyl floors. I pass countless numbered doors. Only one is open: to a room of legless and armless dummies set up on the floor for a CPR training. No one is there. As I walk past various laboratories and offices, I wonder how much debt I will incur with this latest round of medical consultations. Will I live to pay it off?

In the Health Sciences Library, I locate the aisle shelved high with cardiology books. I make my way through a slew of titles such as *Cardiovascular Disease, Pharmacology of the Failing Heart, Spatial Vectocardiography,* and *Myocardial Diseases* to the two shelves on cardiomyopathy. I scan the collection for an up-to-date cardiology textbook, but I can't find one printed within the last decade. I spot a general guide for laypeople from 1997 and then a brand-new heart physiology textbook that includes a chapter on the molecular biology of overload hypertrophy. Bingo. Later I will review it with my Eurythmist friend, Ann, who happens to be staying with me. She worked as a nurse in cardiac care for years and helps me follow the etiology of "deformational changes in the microarchitecture."

Walking through the library with these hefty books, I think of my great-grandfather, Doc, once a research fellow himself, who frequented medical stacks of an earlier generation. Would he have been intrigued by an electric stethoscope, amazed to have access to echocardiograms? Would he argue, as some in medicine do, that reliance on this technology has interfered with doctors' ability to directly perceive heart symptoms? I wonder about his manner when he had to give his patients bad news.

Well-armed with my selection, I make my way down the stairs and out into the blazing day. At the bus stop, I stand in the shade of an Atlas cedar as cars whiz by. I keep a lookout for my bus, too dazed to open any of my books. On the bus, I try to read—after all, that's what I like about this transport, but my eyes blur with tears. I look out the window. We stop by a church with a placard that says, "Great oaks were once nuts that stood their ground." This heartens me, having chosen the name "Oak," knowing that I can add standing my ground to what I will need to see me through, along with grace and stoutness. I think of my great-grandmother, Mary-Cushing, the Christian Scientist, who stood in the ground of her faith, secure in spiritual cure.

When I get home, I open the door and our tortoise cat, Sophie, dashes in, carrying a small dead bird in her mouth. I shudder and tears fill my eyes. I scoop her up so she can devour the poor creature outside. But when I move her, the bird falls from her mouth and flutters. Sophie resists me and struggles to get back to her prey, but I run outside with her, set her down, and close the door quickly, desperate to get back to the injured bird.

I return to where the bird had been dropped on the floor and find an empty space. For the next five minutes I search everywhere, beginning with looking under things to see if it crawled to a safe dark place to die. Satisfied that the bird isn't in the house anymore, I return to the dining room, where I notice a partially open window and look out for a fallen bird. Breathing deeply, I feel my heart pound with its extra *whoosh*. I stand still, amazed that the bird found its way out, well enough to fly free.

∾

*October, 2004*
*Seattle*

## Man of Heart

A mask I made hangs above the window, shiny layers of tissue paper in emerald green with a gold heart around his mouth. Who is this heart-full being? It is Gawan, from Wolfram von Eschenbach's classic, *Parzival*. I have worked with this Grail legend as a storyteller, both telling it and teaching about its archetypal significance, for years now. This hero expresses the positive powers of the planet Mars: champion knight upholding the good, true, and beautiful; passionate lover, imbued with vitality. I relish telling of Gawan surmounting obstacles and overcoming ordeals. A verb, this man.

Since our first walk, David and I have met a few times. We are sitting over tea and I notice his eyes are green. Imagine my surprise when he tells me, "My spiritual practice is to rest into my heart. I've discovered my mind is just a monkey on my back. I thank it for its ability to calculate, but it's not reliable for much else." And I feel the gush of warmth aglow in the space under my breastbone.

It is as simple and profound as that. No mystery schools or initiations, no gurus or esoteric studies: just centering into a depth of calm heart, entering into being present to the moment. I know that this is not theoretical, because I experience this in him, through his strength and radiance of presence, pure and direct. When we begin to spend time together, my mask of Gawan keeps falling off the wall by the mantel where it has hung for months. Each time I retrieve it, I almost hear those golden lips whisper, "You are done with me! Recognize that there is a man in your life that embodies what you have been longing for."

❧

*Late Winter – Spring, 2005*
*Seattle*

## Unveiling

It is winter. In my customary solitude, I have a dream: an old woman is in heavy nun's robes that have to do with her being widowed more than because of religious vows. How long has she been in mourning? Ages! She has a shawl wrapped around her face, mummy-like, with only the barest of slits for her eyes. Little disks of lenses rest on these openings. There is a sense that this shrouding has been required. There is a gentleman visitor with her (that archaic term is in accord with how he is portrayed) who is warm and solicitous. He tells her that he is the same age as her and suggests that they have much in common. A potential courtship is hinted at, implied. In response to his interest, she begins very slowly to unwrap the shawl that has been hiding her for so long, allowing her hair and her face to be revealed. She is radiant, full of joy to shed her old habit.

It is early spring and this is not a dream: I am with a man whom I am growing to be fond of as a friend. Slowly we build trust and open towards intimacy. We sit by the lake beside a cottonwood tree that buds out in vibrant green against the Seattle grays we've grown accustomed to. Over the months that we have gradually been getting to know one another, we keep realizing how much we have in common. Today by the gently lapping water, he tells me that I seem to always to be draped, hiding my body in scarves and layers of flowing clothes, that he has no idea of the actual shape of my body. Why am I hiding? he asks. I can't remember the last time a man wanted to see my body. I laugh and tell him that he is on to something: my Sufi name was "Batina," which means "the veiled one"—one of the ninety-nine attributes of God: to remain hidden.

I haven't used the name "Batina" in decades. Remembering my dream and taking his comment as a dare to reveal myself, I take stock of my wardrobe and habits. I have a multitude of scarves and usually wear one around my neck, knotted above my heart in a protective gesture over full blouses and long skirts or baggy slacks. I am still dressing in the motherly manner I have become accustomed to from years of full belly and nursing. The next time that I go shopping for clothes, I make sure I find a closer fitting shirt.

It begins with shedding baggy pants, scarves, and loose blouses and proceeds to other ways of revealing myself. There are so many layers to let fall in response to his interest. As we grow closer, I cast away encrustations and defenses set in place to protect me from love's injuries. It takes time to realize that I am not being attacked and no longer need that armoring.

It is later in the spring when I welcome his undressing me. As we become involved, men from my past suddenly contact me out of the blue, apologizing for the hurt they caused. This too is a shedding, as wound after wound is dislodged from my heart. Gradually, I dare the contours of exposure, stripping down to raw stark truth. I am no longer an old woman in mourning, no longer enshrouded.

❧

*June, 2005*
*Seattle*

## Cardiac Consultation XIII: Demolition

Summer solstice. Last night, we celebrated the expanse of light as we overlooked the sound, watching the sun spread a golden path across the waters as it sunk lower and lower behind the mountains in pure splendor. We searched for a word for that majestic shimmering light and offered up our gratitude for the source of life and the myriad graces that abound for us. "We" is David and me—his deepening presence in my life is primary among blessings for me of late. I'm still not sure what to call him either, this new man in my life. My lover? My boyfriend? Another unnamed path of gold. Today he's driven me to Harborview Hospital again for a follow-up consultation a week after my first annual transthoracic echo that was prescribed to keep track of how the HCM may be progressing, a year after my re-diagnosis.

I am used to facing these medical procedures and consultations alone, time and time again braced for confronting the medical establishment's cold calculations. That hard hardiness in me
comes from my mother, who braved going alone to receive her
chemo injections as she was dying of metastasized breast cancer.
She drove an hour each way every week for over a year, even when
she could barely stand anymore. Early on in her treatment, I visited, and when she refused my offer to take her, I understood that
respecting her self-sufficiency was the support she wanted. This is
the mould I am breaking free from as David accompanies me. To
have a caring companion can soften the edges. The warmth flowing between our hands is a huge distraction from the suffering
that surrounds us. We both sigh as a stretcher passes by with an
unconscious elderly man being rushed somewhere.

Last week, I showed David an introductory booklet on my
heart condition and pointed out the misshapen cardiac structure.
Ashamed of my defect, I fretted over having him witness this in
me so closely. But I have begun to take in how willing he is to see
me and see me through. In the echo lab, cardiology posters adorn
the walls—diagrams pointing out deviations from a normal heart.
Set aside from these technical pictures, David pointed out a small
framed print of a figurative heart with a pen piercing through it,
above a mysterious word in calligraphy—Latin?—that we didn't
recognize, nor did the sonographers who were doing the sound-
probe of my heart. An entire heart skewed on a pen and not a drop
of blood, invoking alchemical imagery, a variation on the heart of
Mary the Madonna, pierced by a sword.

On this overcast day, David's eyes twinkle blue-gray. He is
beside me again to meet with Dr. Stout, my preferred cardiologist

from the original team that saw me last year. She is as perky as I remember, around forty I guess, with an air of enthusiasm, forthright confidence, and ease. My mounting apprehension kept me awake last night, the shortest night of the year. A foreboding in the way the echo was performed, sensing that something was amiss— again. Not that I have at all been feeling poorly. Two days ago, David took me out to the mountains to Boulder Creek. We hiked up to spectacular falls that rushed down a rock face of a hundred feet or so, green with moss and ferns. I needed to sit down to rest after awhile, but had no heart symptoms. We must have walked four or five miles, although it was rather ambling at times.

Dr. Stout is incredulous to hear of this hike. In fact, she is surprised that I am not having difficulty walking up a flight of stairs. "There is a total disconnect between the test results and your lack of symptoms." She goes over the echo results that alarm her—the force of blood in my left ventricle that calculates to an extraordinary increase of pressure inside my heart. She qualifies this as life threatening, although I am clear of four of the other five factors of high risk for sudden death. She tells us this is the highest velocity she has ever seen, bar none. I am scribbling down notes as she goes into the necessity, in her estimation, of taking an aggressive approach. She recommends implanting a defibrillator to take over if my heart succumbs to electrical instability. "Otherwise I will lie awake at two in the morning and worry about you."

I notice the necklace she has on, a delicate enameled heart, shaped a bit differently than a typical figurative heart, its curves swollen. She suggests that I do a stress echocardiogram soon, which can measure what happens to my blood pressure while I exercise on a treadmill. If the pressure drops, it will verify the severity of the need to intervene, but if it increases, a healthy response, it actually doesn't rule out the possibility of … David hears the term again: sudden death. He hasn't faded yet. She adds that she will need to be there with me while I do the test, in case I collapse.

She writes out a name on a card and tells me to line up a consultation with the electrophysiologist, to start the process of getting an ICD—an Implantable Cardioverter Defibrillator— even though I have doubt. (Just this week, five hundred thousand defibrillators have been recalled due to a short-circuiting malfunction.) She advises getting the financial assistance in place to help cover the expense, knowing that I have visited her here at the clinic she comes to once a month because it takes into account "income sensitivity" and offers a sliding scale. My insurance coverage is only for catastrophic illnesses, and therefore doesn't cover these visits. However, Dr. Stout informs us that no insurance will cover defibrillators, at fifty to seventy thousand dollars a pop. Fifty to seventy thousand dollars! Both David and I are stunned. That's more than the higher education loan I am just starting to pay off at a hundred dollars monthly for thirty years! I laugh and say that decides it. Not an option for me. But even as I say this, Coyote, the trickster, is listening.

Dr. Stout is adamant that I take care of myself, avoiding all stress. She implores me not go on anymore hikes whatsoever and warns against my being out of range of emergency rooms. I appreciate her generous response to my request for references to explore about recent HCM research by showing me some Internet sources for core clinical journals. Then she asks to have a listen to the source of all this alarm. She bends down and places the listening plate of her coiled stethoscope over my heart. She pauses and shifts it to another position and listens attentively again. As she stands up, she looks rather puzzled, "I am surprised not to hear a more intense gradient. I wouldn't have expected that." David's gray eyes flash me an inquiring glance.

Dr. Stout admits that there is "a gray zone component" to my case. She says that she will be checking in with her colleagues because these findings are so unique. It turns out that she has a connection with the researcher at the Mayo Clinic that Dr. McKenna in England recommended to me as reputable. His specialty is surgery, which has improved dramatically in precision and outcome in the last decade. Not that I would consider that level of brutal intervention.

At the end of our consultation, Dr. Stout leads us to a computer in another room. A doctor who has been viewing my echo stands up abruptly as we enter, commenting that it is all set up for us to see. She points out areas of concern to us, but they are all a blur to me. I believe her. In the hallway, I nestle into the shelter of David's arms and my tears begin to flow. He holds me close.

Eventually, I pull away, sniffling. David unfolds his neatly folded handkerchief to pat my tears. We are too stunned for words. Instead, we watch the demolition of the old hospital building across the street. Barely anything remains of the once-elegant brick building that for so long was a permanent fixture here on "Pill Hill." No wrecking ball is in sight. David is fascinated by the crane-like machine's ability to be maneuvered to rip apart sections of the building—walls and ceilings dismantled by the mechanized teeth taking bites of mortar. Mouthfuls of steel rebar lie mangled in a pile next to the heap of battered concrete, hosed down to reduce dust. We gaze at deconstruction. The entire building is gone except for an elevator surrounded by the absence of all that it once opened to. The medical building is in ruins. Rain begins to fall on rubble.

In the car, before driving anywhere, we debrief. David rages a bit, unwinding from holding it together. "I wanted to take you to the trees to heal your heart and now she's saying you have to stay in the city?!" We agree that until the stress echo, I am pretty much in limbo. I tell him I could never have a machine implanted in me, that no way would I choose to become robotic. The rain falls harder as we drive away.

✌⃝

*Summer, 2005 – Summer, 2007*
*Seattle*

## Taking Aim

David accompanies me to the stress echo and cheers me on as I walk into a jog on the treadmill. Will I be okay? The echocardiogram is tracking my heart as I quicken my pace. What will this inside view of my heart under exertion reveal? The speed of the electrical walkway picks up as the incline increases. My legs, unused to running, are weak after six minutes—but my heart keeps steady. Although the technicians are not allowed to give us any results, let alone interpretation, David watches carefully. He is able to tell that my blood pressure doesn't fall, and we are both relieved, since that was the primary danger Dr. Stout wanted to rule out. But since I can't afford to see her except in the low-income, sliding scale clinic, it will be another six weeks until we will find out what it all means. That time becomes an interlude of unrest for me. I am uneasy knowing that my heart's function, measured and recorded, is kept unknown.

David is there at my side again in early August, for Dr. Stout's report (finally!). According to the echo, my heart responded fairly well. The fact that my blood pressure did not increase during exercise is a good outcome, and another one is that, much to her surprise, the velocity of my outflow track decreased as well. However, my blood pressure decreased after exercise—not a regular response. She admits that these results are mystifying. In fact, she took my case to a whole team of cardiologists at a conference recently. They all agreed that it is a "gray area."

Dr. Stout tells us that she doesn't think it is dire now that I get a defibrillator implanted, although she still encourages me to consider it and meet with the electrophysiologist to "get the ball rolling." She reluctantly respects me when I tell her I am not interested at all. She ends by reminding me, "HCM is fluid and variable. Your case is unique." She advises me to pay attention and listen to my body—keep hydrated, don't over-exert myself; know my limits: rest when I need to rest, and keep getting checked. Of course: an echo every year.

I carry home my notes and underline her statement that, "There is not necessarily a correlation between the severity of the gradient (velocity) and the electrical instability that causes sudden death." Rereading them, I laugh, recognizing that David, an electrician by trade, has become my stability.

The following June, David and I are happy as we begin to make a home together. I am still paying monthly for my consultation with Dr. Stout. I let my annual follow-up echocardiogram slide. This is not as a fully conscious decision. Why deal with the medical model that only points to mechanical fixes if my condition worsens? Why measure it at all? I am doing fine and have already clearly chosen not to pursue that route. Isn't it my prerogative to let it be?

As I let it be, a second year will pass without an echocardiogram. I will avoid getting up suddenly out of bed or walking downstairs when I've been sleeping because my heart rate goes so high. I will be accustomed to weariness, finding it necessary to take a nap every day. I will weep when I find I am not strong enough to work for more than half an hour at a time in the garden. I will avoid riding a bike. I will refrain from walking too far around the lake. I will be enraged when a colleague at the high school where I teach tells me that they've decided not to give me any more classes to teach, " ... because we are afraid if you take on any more, you might keel over and die ... "

But I will not be aware of Artemis taking aim; I will not hear the arrow whirring towards me at full speed.

᠆ᡣᠣ

*Rhode Island, 1960s*
*Seattle, late 1990s*

## Guardian

As a child, every summer included visiting my great-uncle in the antique house that my great-grandparents had built, far from city's grumble. In a room that looked out over the Pawcatuck River, I slept under a sepia portrait. In soft lines, a man in loose robes with long hair and a beard, his face slightly turned with kind eyes, smiled down on me. When I awoke in hushed darkness, golden light poured out of his gaze, a calm radiance that bathed me with peace. There was nothing in my outer life to frame this experience, since Quakerism, the religion I was raised in, was opposed to icons. I am not sure at what age I identified this comforting being as Jesus. I never mentioned this first brush with grace, but it stayed with me, pure.

Sometime between visiting the offices of Zenith Cardiology at Northwest Hospital and being a patient there, years later, I had a striking dream infused with the same vibrant radiance of spirit that I had known as a child. My dream was simply of being discharged after surgery from Northwest. I was walking through a massive parking garage and suddenly, I knew that Christ was with me, not as a figure, but as a vibrant healing presence. The same effulgence I had known as a child carried into waking. I had no idea where the dream had come from, and was curious as to why such a potent grace would be associated with a specific place—and why a hospital? Those images and the grace I had tasted stayed with me, a reference point to call upon over a decade later when I went to be hospitalized there.

It was a solace I would need.

*October, 2007*
*Seattle*

## Surgery Sequence

### I. Remodel

In the heavily overcast dawn, as I strip down for surgery, I recall Inanna. In an ancient Sumerian myth, when she prepares to leave "the great above for the great below," Inanna arranges her hair across her forehead and dons her regalia—her crown, a small lapis necklace on her throat, a double strand of beads on her breast— and wraps her royal robe around her. She puts on her breastplate and gold ring, and takes her lapis measuring rod and line in her hand. Gate by gate in her descent, each of these is removed from her. It's a story I know by heart. I've told it in story-circles and classrooms. At each gate when something is stripped away, she cries out, "What is this?" and is told, "Quiet, Inanna, the ways of the Underworld are perfect; they may not be questioned." But she keeps asking at each of the seven gates, until naked and bowed low, she enters the throne room of her sister, Ereshkigal. There she is struck by the eye of death and hung on a meat hook for three days: an ancient crucifixion.

My fingers feel odd without the rings I have worn for so long, and even my silver star toe-ring needs to be removed. David has taken my coat to the car, and alone now in a curtained cubicle with a rolling bed, I undress. Naked, I fold my hands over my heart and bow slightly in surrender. I glance at my intact chest one last time before donning the light green gown with busy blue lines and red squiggles. Versions of this will become my uniform in the next week and I will get to know all its openings, snaps, and ties to maneuver around tubes. A nurse asks, "Ready?" and when I assent, she opens the curtains and tells me to lie down. She places a heated blanket on me. I try not to think of how during the surgery they will lower my body temperature severely to induce hypothermia. I won't let myself dwell on the image of cold salt water being poured on my heart, but I can't help but notice it's the same composition as tears.

David returns, holds my hand and reassures me with his loving gaze. The pre-surgery bustle begins with Dr. C, the anesthesiologist, introducing himself. He begins an IV of Versed (to forget) and my awareness dims accordingly. Another gate in my descent. The assistant surgeon joins us and makes small talk. Dr. V arrives in his scrubs with a cheery "good morning" and tells me that in going over my echo again, it looks more likely that my mitral valve will have to be replaced. He doesn't say "cut out." I am given more papers to sign and they harness me into the bed. David stoops over, his lips finding mine in a long, slow, time-stopping kiss, before he takes leave. His taste lingers. I know he'll be waiting nearby.

My glasses are taken. Everything is a blur. Sounds muffle and din.

My body strapped down, I rise up from Earth's hold. I become the light princess in the story I loved in my childhood. Unencumbered, I float. Instead of being held by the ribbons of courtiers, I am corded with tubes and wires. My consciousness is erased while my body is chilled down and operated upon. There are more gates to pass through in my descent: breath circumvented, circulation rerouted.

*Jolt.* Out of erasure into the blear of sedation, I still can't see, although I sense David nearby. After thirty hours of lying unconscious in Texas, I am used to knowing him in the dim—as tone, as sensed presence, his radiant heart a guidepost. As soon as I open my eyes, he is ready to tell me that I am in the ICU, that the surgery was a success. The hand I love above all others strokes my forehead. My lungs are being squeezed—open, shut. There are other hoses draining from me, and wires connecting me to a monitor. I am being breathed by a machine. I try to find my chest. How is it? Too far away to know.

Over the next few days, my awareness vacillates between semi and complete stupor. I have my glasses now, but what takes place in the ICU is just a veneer, beneath which, as soon as I close my eyes, another world is revealed. It begins with the same void I experienced in Humble: dense black with pulsating points of light, as if I am peering into cellular structures, galactic and subatomic in one. Not just visual, but dizzying, this gravity of oblivion. As long as I keep my eyes open, I won't fall in?

I vomit and bleed. With effort, I press the button to raise or lower my bed. I can't sit myself. I drift between worlds. I can't stay awake while Betsy visits with a gift of orange mountain ash berries, of crimson oak leaves, to bring nature in to me. David hangs them nearby, a dash of color in the sterile room where flowers are forbidden. I learn the nurses' names. I forget them. Blood is drawn from me every four hours, IV's checked, replaced. David tells me things. I can't keep track. My friend Laurie says words; I nod and they fade.

The respirator has been removed. My breath is shallow, but my own. There is a plastic mask of oxygen over my face. I could speak now, if only I could form the words. To string them together demands a rigor I do not yet possess. But I mumble: "Lethargic … " To find the word to describe my condition is a supreme accomplishment. I have drunk deeply of Lethe, the spring of the Underworld, of forgetfulness. My eyes shut despite my effort to keep them wide open. It is useless.

Behind my lids, I enter a different realm. I have lost track of how many gates I have passed through. Surely this is subterranean. Beings melt one into another, grasping, jabbering, crying out in anguish. They are hurt. They are tormented, molten, distorted, entrapped, cruel. This toll of misery keeps moving—suffering, suffering, suffering, suffering. Later I will recognize it as hell. Hell's dancing. The nine circles of Dante's inferno crisscrossed and jumbled. Later, when I can say what I saw, Laurie will recognize my visions as *bardos*, intermediary states between death and birth.

Liminal. Meanwhile, I try hard to keep my eyes open. When I don't, I sink back into the swirls of ghoulish agony.

Then I am awake, alone with the glow of machines interrupting the dark.

I don't know when the oxygen mask was taken off; there are tubes in my nostrils now. My breathing is shallow. I am lying on my back, slightly propped up. I can feel a little steady jolting inside me, against my back. I veer away from going any further into the sensation, understanding that in order to be comfortable, I will need to ignore this. I carefully maneuver to lie on my right side, facing the tube of my IV and the line of the morphine drip that I can self-administer when I want, by squeezing. I hardly use it, preferring pain to the blankness.

Slowly I move my tethered hands to my chest. They rest on the bandaging between my breasts, thickly taped up to my collarbone, and ending somewhere else out of sight, indeterminable. In a rush of gentleness, my awareness reaches into the wound below the wad. Tears flow in gratitude mingling with the pain, not unlike the time after giving birth. I want to comfort this newborn, raw and fragile. I want to cheer her on, "You made it!" I want to soothe what has been cut. I remember the line from the Aramaic version of the Lord's Prayer. "Soften the ground of our being and carve out a space within us where your presence can abide." I recognize that this is literal now, in my case: this carving out of my flesh that has created a new shape: hollowed heart, hallowed ground.

## II. Post Surgery

"Love heals," Susan, our day nurse tells us, smiling, "this I know." She is gently washing my face, dipping a cloth in a basin of warm water, washing away the sweat from my latest drench. The sound of the water being wrung out is soothing. She has made a point of letting us know, as almost every nurse has, how David and I are quite the team. Although there is the barrier of my fragility between me and him, there is communion in our glance.

I am still in the ICU, my third day here. Imprisoned. The windows are sealed shut. Oh, for a breath of fresh air! Not that I can breathe very well, anyway. One of the things that keeps me busy here is un-collapsing my lungs by inhaling into an incentive spirometer, a plastic device that measures "inspiratory volume." I must do ten breaths every hour. I place my mouth around a flexible tube that connects to a chamber where a plunger rises up along the marks of millimeters in blue from zero to two thousand and fifty. On the other side, there is a blue indicator. I must attempt to keep it between two arrows, by remaining steady in my output. David and Laurie and Susan take turns coaching me in this major exertion. "C'mon, Mary." Ten breaths: interminable. I can't go any deeper than my diaphragm and can't draw my usual deeper belly breaths. At the end, I hug a pillow to support my incision while forcibly coughing to clear my lungs. Then I rest from the exertion.

Yesterday, my drain tube was taken out from under my ribs with a huge slither and plop. My catheter was also removed. Each shift of position requires effort. I've been instructed in how to turn and sit without using my hands, how to heave myself up rounding around the pillow pressed against my chest. David or a nurse hoists me up with a "one-two-three!" My first destination was to the commode.

Today, David drapes an extra hospital gown around me and, with him wheeling my IV, I walk. He is counting: one step, pause, another. We have time. I shuffle on. When we reach the nursing station, a cheer rises up from bright faces. One step, pause, another. All the doors are open. In the next room over from mine, an elderly Indian man is dying, with his family keeping vigil. In a low voice, David tells how there have been people surrounding him continuously, a clan sleeping in the waiting room always accompanied by a bounty of curry-scented food. One step, pause, another. In the other rooms of the telemetry unit, people lie alone: blank stares, the blare of television, and a cacophony of coughs— rattling, hacking, barking.

To take each step, I must summon all my strength. I wish I could walk as far as the fire escape, to breathe some fresher air. But: not yet. I return to my lair. After my grand excursion, I am relieved to go back to bed. I have been off the heavy-duty pain-killers since yesterday, much to everyone's surprise. That has been the biggest relief. But I am exhausted.

When I close my eyes, there is still a continuous whirl of images. Thankfully, the flames have subsided. Now: caves and grottos, rainforest trails with rich earth and ferns, streambeds with flowing waters, rocky riverbeds with currents cascading, rocky gullies with surging waters, stone conduits with waters gushing. For days I see variations of these pathways, ever-moving and mobile. I may not have access to being out in nature, but this is the dance of the elements taking place in my body, Pistis Sophia condensing spirit into dynamic constituents shaping substance, form, and structure. My heart, with its added trough, is growing accustomed to its new pathway of circulation.

### III. Implantation

With a dry mouth, I am waiting. Five days since my first surgery. My ICD will be implanted sometime tomorrow, possibly in the morning, so I am not allowed to have food or drink: NPO is written in bold letters on the door: *nil per os* (nothing by mouth). It is three in the morning and I haven't been able to fall asleep since my last vital sign check. I am proud of myself for doing the incentive spirometer on my own. I am thirsty. Hours later, I will be given a tiny sponge on a stick that I can dip in water and swab my mouth with. That will make it almost bearable.

I am in dread. I don't want to have wires run through my flesh and attach to my heart, let alone pace it. I've been told that in heart surgery it is common for the sinoatrail node, which controls the electrical systems of the heart, to be damaged, so the ICD must take over its natural pacing. The best-case scenario is that the ICD would only be a back up if/when a dangerous rhythm occurs. Time will tell.

When the pale of day comes, I am told that the surgery won't happen in the morning after all. The actual time hasn't yet been set. Still: NPO. I am moved from the ICU, down the hall to another room. This one has an open view, and relief spreads through me—just to see the sky. Over the stretch of the flat graveled roof below, there is a grand oak tree, aflame in the October drizzle. I sit in a chair facing out and let my eyes absorb the colors. I try to ignore how dry my mouth is. I find the box of colored pencils and the sketchbook I brought along and begin to draw. First, with many shades of green: a wing. It is my way of summoning Raphael, the archangel of healing. I am trying to take my trepidation and transform it into the gesture of enfolding. I pray for protection with each stroke of the pencil. Then I draw the tree in its golden hues.

I am so thirsty.

After waiting all day, I am wheeled away to surgery in the late afternoon. David walks alongside. They tell him it will be a brief procedure, a simple one—forty-five minutes or so, and that I will be out in about an hour, by six o'clock. I don't want to say goodbye and my lips are too parched to give a real kiss. I squeeze his hand hard and smile bravely.

The anesthesiologist is a cheery young woman whose name slips away as soon as she tells me. I admire her cap, made of fabric adorned with pumpkins. She made it herself, she tells me, one way to be original—she has them for each season. As a matter of fact, most of the crew has their own style of cap along with their scrubs. Vivid colors infiltrate a sterile place. She tells me since it's a short operation, I won't need as much anesthesia as before, so my reaction should be more favorable. As she begins to look for a place to insert the IV, I warn her that everyone has been having trouble finding my veins.

"No problem," she dismisses me. After a few futile attempts, she succeeds—with a great splatter of blood all over her. As soon as the tube is in place, with Verced slowly oozing into me, she excuses herself to change her clothes, since she now looks more like a butcher than a doctor.

I ask for one last swab for my arid mouth. My glasses are taken away, and I am in the operating room, amazed at the brightness of the overhead lights, the sheen of stainless steel. From where I lie on my back, I check out all I didn't remember from before, as if I could grasp hold while my awareness begins to slip away. I can't. A couple of assistants introduce themselves and strap my arms down. Dr. W arrives. Touching my left shoulder, he confidently goes over what they will be doing. His words blur and fade. I am drifting off, lifting away. There is a current that I recognize, flowing from a woman to my right. Although I can't make out her features, her smile is luminous. She is praying for me—isn't she? Or is it an angel shining through ?

*I am a child at the ocean shore, waves crashing. I am flying my butterfly kite for the first time, for the last. Painted rice paper*

*stretched over bamboo framing, complete with antennae. The winds
lift it further from me, into a dark sky.*

*I become the kite, bright colors in breeze, floating, fluttering,
suddenly lifted by a gust, untethered.*

*No, I must not rise any farther ...*

*With a yank, I become the child again, scared by the leap of
the string, unexpectedly reeling off its spool, unwound and released.
I cry out, grasping for the kite string, just beyond my reach ... no,
this cannot be ... does it hover and return, that slight string? I jump
and somehow grasp it, I pull with all my might ... Or is it me, being
heaved back?*

*Jolt.* Erasure fades. Voices. I am in breath, in a post-op room.
Someone is holding my hand. I murmur "hello" and the three
women around me move closer in, greeting me. One of them slips

me my glasses. The one holding my hand is beaming at me with intense compassion, the darshan of a holy person. When I ask how it went, they look at one another and an agreement passes between them, "Dr. W will give you a full report ..." I am given my glasses and once I put them on, I notice over three hours have passed.

Through my grog, I ask, "Is it really 8:30?"

I am answered with a look that I can't read, "We're taking you back to your room now."

They wheel me down a hall, past windows. It is completely dark outside. Late. As soon as I am wheeled out through the automated doors, David rushes over to me. He touches me with relief and tenderness. "Am I glad to see you!" he exclaims.

"How come it's so late?" I ask, muzzy.

"I'll tell you all about it when we get back to the room."

As the hours drew out, David had known something was wrong. He had been pacing by the time Dr. W finally appeared, looking down and shaking his head.

"She's all right ... " he said, shaken, "... but we almost lost her."

David is stroking my forearm as he relays what happened. He tells me how he was impressed by Dr. W's vulnerability, his concern. "I never liked the idea of them stopping your heart to test the defibrillator. It turns out that they had trouble starting it again." The standard procedure is to implant the defibrillator and then test it, increasing the voltage each time. I can't follow all the words my electrician sweetheart uses—joules failing to convert, and such. The translation is: my heart didn't respond to the defibrillator and they had to use external paddles to shock me back, not once, but three times, and "it was touch and go for awhile."

That night, David stays with me on a cot as close to my bed as we can move it, with the side railing down so we can hold hands. He is the kite handle from which I won't unwind.

## IV. Butterfly Valve

Over a week has passed and I am still in the telemetry unit, waiting. I have laughed at how being a hospital patient demands patience and have cried, not finding that quality in myself, cooped in as I am. Guests, nurses, phlebotomists, doctors all get to leave and return. I must remain so my heart can be continually monitored. Waiting. I have grown accustomed to fragmented sleep, to all the intrusions and pokes—blood draws, IV changes. I gaze out the window and witness autumn's palette scribed in the leaf changes of oak, of cottonwoods. I watch the light of passing hours. I long for my captivity to cease.

There is weight in the waiting.

We await the thinning of my blood. There is danger since my bloodstream would naturally clot around the valve that is newly in place in my left ventricle. At the nurses' desk there is a sample of a porcine valve—made from grafting a pig's heart, a natural membrane that isn't rejected in the same way. I pick it up and examine it, preserved in a clear plastic block, with its threefold pinkish leaflets, a strange bioprosthetic flower. It's the valve that I don't have. It wasn't even a question for me, I am told, because its durability is only for about fifteen years. I am considered young enough that it would need to be replaced—"we wouldn't want to have to open you up again!" So I have a valve of titanium. The only drawback to my nickel-sized contraption is that it requires blood-thinning, which makes me a borderline hemophiliac. David tells me how a butterfly valve works—but the mechanics escape me, as I focus on its namesake, hoping psyche portends redemption.

Patient education: we're given instructions about Warfarin, the drug that interacts with my liver to change the chemistry of my blood. Video presentations, handbooks. Regularity in one's diet, one's sleep. Rhythm, balance. Parameters I must strive for the rest of my life. We await the right ratio between bleed and clot. Then I can go home.

Meanwhile, on this golden clear morning, Mary Scarlett has arranged a special treat: I can get disconnected from the heart monitor for a spell and go out. As in: outside; as in: fresh air! I am bundled up in a wheelchair and trundled outside by David and Laurie. The vivid astonishment of chill, the scent and rustle of fallen leaves, sunlight on my face. Relief in my senses' yearning quenched in pure refreshment. Laurie walks beside as David wheels me around the campus of the arboreal hospital. I am intensely aware of newly naked birch and beech, of cherry and cedar, of the green of plants—salal, ferns, and other nameless shrubs, as I meet them in breath.

David parks me by a fountain, and my companions sit down on patio chairs nearby. My ears delight in the gush and surge of water. Laurie whips out blank 3 x 5 cards and pens and invites us to write haiku. I laugh, and breathe in the moment.

> *Gift of elements*
> *Water flowing over stones*
> *Air dances sunlight*

*Clapping water falls*
*Applause for the heart renewed.*

—David

The next morning, my blood is stabilized enough to go home. The IV nurse comes for the last time and removes the portal to my bloodstream. I am signed out, untethered from the monitor for good, as if I am done here. As if I won't need this access for a very long time.

## V. Return

After ten days in the ICU and telemetry unit, I am home again, on St. Jude's feast day. The new high-tech bio-gadget wired into me is referred to as "a St. Jude," the patron saint of hospital workers, lost causes and last resorts. That covers my situation fairly well. Relieved, I savor the textures and colors of the non-hospitalized world, enjoying the flowers that are permitted here, my children's paintings on the walls—a red lion, a deep well, a rainbow, and the photos of dear ones collaged around the light switch, beloved books surrounding me. The solace of our bed, my body as fragile as it is, curled into David's—toe to toe, nose to neck, breath to breath.

Recuperating reminds me of the times after giving birth, everything reduced to basic physical acts: sleeping, eating, shitting (or not), drinking, peeing, and gingerly moving. Instead of bonding with a new infant, I am bonding with my remodeled heart. I am getting used to the incision that slices from just below my collar bone down between my breasts. David calls this mar my battle scar, reassuring me that it is beautiful. Each night: the joy of touching and of lovingly being touched. No bars between us.

Each day: tears. My range is so limited—the steps are steep and I have to take them one at a time, my sternal precautions keeping my range of reach quite limited, getting out of a flat bed is a major feat. But David is there, feeding and lifting me in tenderness and patience. I rest, mostly, moving from bed to couch. Sometimes when I fall asleep, I am woken up by a primal whimper—my own.

Each time I go out for a stroll, I amble further. I can't quite call it a walk yet, because I am so slow. But each day there is a bit more spring in my saunter, slightly more ease in exertion. Deeper breath. Progress.

Until:

Later in the week, everything becomes more strenuous. My blood is seriously thin, over double its therapeutic range, and they keep decreasing my dose of Warfarin in order to get it down. Walking arm and arm in the wind, David tells me, "You seem like a heart patient again today," worried to see how I have re-debilitated. We are bundled up at Golden Gardens, where a couple of days ago, I accomplished a modest distance, a measure of increasing strength. Today, I can barely make it from one bench to another. What is wrong? Woozy and weak, by the time I drag myself to bed, I begin to vomit. Every hour all night: retching, which compounds the pain in my sternum. My breath is constricted, my diaphragm compressed. By morning I can't even stand. Everything is spinning around me.

At the ER, I am weak with the effort of waiting to be admitted. As soon as the nurse on duty feels my pulse, she puts me in a wheelchair and rushes me into a room. I lie back on the bed and float in surrender to being here, where I will be taken care of. The sense of peace I feel contrasts with the commotion around me: a sudden team of people around us when the monitor shows my heart is in atrial fibrillation. With a furrowed brow, David squeezes my hand. They are getting out the paddles ... but then, suddenly, my heart settles to a normal rhythm. The doctor congratulates me on not having to be cardioverted, as if he could tell that my prayer was answered. I drift into the relief of discovering what is wrong, and to dealing with it. Tests are ordered to see deeper into my heart: an X-ray, an echo.

Back in a hospital gown of green with blue squiggles, up in the ICU, in Room #316, the very same room I awoke in from my surgery weeks ago, I lie in bed with David sitting beside me, again. We are happy to see Mary Scarlett's familiar face, her green eyes bordered by chestnut hair. She has pulled up a chair, rare for her to stop and sit. A necklace of bronze hearts and agates is framed by her lily-white coat today. She has my test results and tells us that since it is a complication of the heart surgery, she is overseeing my care. "It turns out that you have quite a large amount of fluid built up in the sac that surrounds your heart, and even in your lungs. No wonder you were feeling so much pressure!" David and I both nod and she continues, "This was probably happening slowly since the surgery and just got to the point where there is so much fluid accumulation that you can't breathe fully and it's squeezing in on your heart as well, which is why you went into A-fib."

It is too strenuous to laugh at how watery I am, my body responding to surgery by filling with fluid, but I smile. I learn the name for this oppression: "pericardial effusion." It isn't until later that I understand that it is also a complication of being anti-coagulated, that the "fluid" is in fact my over-thinned blood. All I know is that I am constricted—I can't breathe easily and I keep throwing up. Mary Scarlett tells us that I will be on plasma to get my blood coagulated enough for surgery. Dr. V will create a little window in my pericardium, and drain the fluid. This will require opening my incision again, but it will not interfere with my sternum. Mary Scarlett shows us where they will make the cut, right below my ribs, and another under my left breast. They will follow this with another procedure the next day to drain my lungs, but not under general anesthesia, to my relief.

I am connected intravenously to a bag of gold plasma. Later, I find out that each bag costs close to a thousand dollars. I remember back to when David gave blood for my initial surgery, a heroic act on his behalf—when we got there, he confessed that needles make him squeamish, but he felt it was the least he could do for me. Next to where he sat to have his blood drawn, there was a man connected to a big, noisy machine. He was obviously comfortable being there. We fell into conversation. He told us that he came regularly for an hours-long procedure to give plasma. Extracting it involves a much more intricate procedure than a straightforward blood draw. Blood flows through a centrifuge, separating out the needed particles, returning the rest. A modern form of alchemy: blood into gold. Little did I know then that I would be a recipient of this *ichor*.

Awaiting the change in blood chemistry so that they can operate takes about twenty-four hours. I am tired and apprehensive about having a hole made in my pericardium—after all, it is a protective membrane, but I am resigned. If only I could stop throwing up!

Hours pass. I doze and drift. David reads the paper, contacts people to let them know of this latest complication. He looks more haggard with every hour. When it is time for him to go, I sincerely wish him well—I am hoping he can sleep a whole night without having to care for me. Tremulously, I steel myself against the dread of being here alone, a raw searing. He stoops over to kiss me as I fumble for equanimity. As he lifts his head away, I whisper "goodbye." The alarm on the heart monitor goes off.

I am in A-fib again, just like that.

By the time the nurses rush in, my heart has calmed. David leaves. Even with Benadryl, and seascape music, I can't unwind into sleep. The golden plasma drips. The monitor hums. *Dear body, I am sorry for all the intrusions thrust upon you once again. I hold you lovingly and ask for the deep wisdom of your instinctual knowing and healing to be responsive to all that is coming your way.* I make an effort to convince myself to relax and trust. But I still can't let go. I am on guard despite my best intentions.

In pre-surgery, the anesthesiologist, a tall, wiry, and worried doctor, is nervous and not open to my request for as light an anesthesia as possible. He dismisses me with a comment about how I have a difficult case already. Not the most assuring thing to hear when I once again need to surrender my consciousness. Dr. V and his assistant come in to say good morning. "Hello, sunshine. I'll take care of this, don't worry." I try, I try. I shudder into surrender. The OR bustle mutes. I unwind into the distance, hours loose, I ascend into blankness.

*Jolt.* Re-entry. A reassuring touch on my forehead, a gentle stroke across my cheek. David is here. He moves close enough so I can see his face clearly, his blue-gray eyes concerned and gentle as he peers at me. His steady gaze helps draw me back here to room 316. Reentering is smoother than from other obliterations. David tells me that they drained 1300 mL (about a quart and a half) of pericardial fluid around my heart and 88 mL of fluid from my left lung, evidently a large amount. Groggy and woozy, but lighter, I am able to breathe again and breathe deep. I sigh, savoring the expanse of out-breath, the depth of taking breath fully in, this steady air stream, no longer constricted.

*November 22, 2007*
*Seattle*

## Thanksgiving Nuptials

> *If the only prayer you ever uttered*
> *was thank you, that would suffice.*
> —Meister Eckhart

Impossible to measure just when our union took place: was it the extended delight opened by touch, the rush of flame, blush and gush of deepening swoon? Was it the conversations that went deep, the tears shared, our moments of mirth, or the way we worked together? Was it the mountain hike we took in high summer up to Twin Falls, still flowing despite the dry days? We had only been lovers a few months then, and although it was becoming more and more difficult to leave one another after passionate nights, we had decided to live through the four seasons before merging households. We sat on the sun-warmed gray basalt, feet in the clear rush of water, wanting to make a plan for our lives that were tumbling by as madly as the river. We rested from the climb and spoke of the desire to find a form, a commitment to the relationship we had created, to avow what we held sacred. We came down from the mountain, knowing we would wed.

Come November, with our wedding planned for Thanksgiving, there was more to celebrate than we had originally had in mind. Despite my cardiac arrest and surgeries, the wedding went forward, simplified. I was released from my final hospitalization just days before our guests began to arrive. Annie, my soul sister from England, had become an interfaith minister, and flew in to officiate. We worked together to create the ceremony, based on some reflecting that David and I had done in preparation.

In the days that followed, there were almost daily drives to the airport to fetch various family members from afar. Old family friends, Alan and Andrea, had graciously opened their home to us to use for the wedding. On Thanksgiving day, while others bustled in our kitchen, Annie, David, David's sister-in-law, and I went to prepare the ceremonial space. In the window seat turned altar, we set peachy-pink and blood-red roses brimming out of a crystal vase, flanked by beeswax tapers. The large window looked out to the eastern horizon, rimmed with the snow-lit Cascades rising above the shimmer of Lake Washington, spread out below.

After our Thanksgiving feast (and a necessary nap for me, still recovering), we return to Andrea's and Alan's. The full moon has risen above the dark expanse of the lake. David and I prepare for the service by lighting a ceremonial fire together, to release any obstacles to our union. Then Annie and I go upstairs—every step an effort for me. She puts on her ritual vestments and helps me put on my simple teal cotton gown. I don the family pearls from my grandmother, and wrap a lace scarf above the padding of my bandages. At the appointed time everyone is gathered expectantly. Descending, I hold on to the railing. David waits, standing across the room. We enter into ritual space, an eternal present. Our eyes meet, we begin, slowly walking a spiral towards one another, accompanied by the tenderest of love songs. We meet in the center, eyes brimming.

Annie stands, priestess radiant, mantled by a stole with sacred symbols embroidered in gold: an OM, a Dharma Wheel, a Star of David, a cross, a crescent and star, a yin/yang symbol. In her warm, inviting voice, she begins an invocation. David and I step towards the altar to light a hefty beeswax candle. I have asked each of my children to invoke a direction, and they rise in a circle to do so.

Broad-shouldered and slightly rumpled, Chris begins in a determined voice, calling in the Spirits of the East, of waking and of freedom, breath of life, and eagle. Kyrian, in pinstripe and purple, fills the space with firm yet effervescent conviction, calling in the Spirits of the South, of vitality and beauty, warmth of fire and stag and salamander. Emmanuel joins, in his double-breasted white suit, steady in his caring as he calls in the Spirits of the West, of fluidity and direction, salmon and otter. Rose in her vintage pink lace dress and golden shoes, finishes, exuberantly inviting the Spirits of the North, of stone and silent owl, to be present with stability and potency.

With blessings interwoven, we are wed. In the silent witness of those we hold most dear surrounding us, we are wed. Enacting the cycle of our shared journey, we are wed. Inviting our children into the circle of our love, we are wed. Garlanded with lei of ti leaf and orchid, rose and kukui nut we are wed. Consecrated in grace, deep gaze, strong grasp, we are wed. Three-fold, seven-fold, nine-fold, twelve—we are wed, one dimension unfolding into another, enfolding us.

෨

*Winter, 2007*
*Seattle*

## Catastrophic Coverage

Everyday my mailbox bulges with medical bills from Texas and various letters from the claims department of my health insurance company. Amidst the complicated codes and abbreviations, this much is clear:

YOUR INSURANCE COMPANY HAS PAID ITS SHARE OF
YOUR BILL. BALANCE IS DIRECTLY PAYABLE BY YOU.

| | |
|---|---|
| Room and Board: | $4,307.00 |
| Intensive Care: | $6,361.00 |
| Hospital Misc: | $52,929.20 |
| Patient Liability: | $50,877.75 |

FULL PAYMENT IS EXPECTED UPON RECEIPT
OF THIS BILL.

What a relief, I thought years ago, to find medical coverage for the self-employed! Rare and welcome, Mega-Life and Health's plan seemed progressive and reasonably priced. A high deductible kept costs down and I had to pay for doctors' visits out of pocket. But I never questioned paying monthly into a policy that would protect my family and me. I assumed "Catastrophic Coverage" was something I could rely on. In the last decade, oblivious to the increase in hospital rates, it never occurred to me to update the plan. But now the explanation of benefits spells out the terms:

*The Health Insurance Plan purchased provides coverage ac-*
*cording to a Schedule of Benefits based on your selected Hospital*
*Room and Board amount. Our records show that you selected the*

*$300.00 per day Hospital Room and Board benefit which also pays Hospital Miscellaneous charges at 80% to a maximum of $15,000. Your claim has been processed according to the terms of your Health Insurance Plan and Benefit Maximums for Hospital Miscellaneous have been paid.*

Bill in my hand, I tremble as I call Patient Financial Services at Kingwood to leave the first of what will become many messages. Eventually, Lavonda returns my call and explains that despite my paltry income, homeowners are not eligible for any kind of help. She makes it clear where my dilemma lies: I will have my house taken if I don't find another way to pay them. In her thick Texan accent she exclaims, "Sorry, Ma'am, that's just the way it is."

Security unravels: I almost lost my body, now I may lose my home of nineteen years. But I have equity in my home. One of my first expeditions out of the house is to my bank. I am not working yet and am not sure how I will cover the higher payment, but I refinance the house to pay off Kingwood.

I become a master at filling out forms. I apply for Medicare. Income verification. Case number. Faxes. I am not eligible since I have squirreled away money every month to pay my real estate taxes, six months worth due soon. I fill out the application from Northwest Hospital Foundation that was given to me, kindly, during my stay. As the bills begin to arrive from Northwest, the expenses of Kingwood look moderate. I worry about having to apply for bankruptcy. I refrain from marrying David legally to prevent dragging him down with me.

During my rehabilitation, David accompanies me to an interview at the Northwest Hospital Foundation. In a little cubicle, we sit with Karen who tells us that my insurance company is no-

torious for taking advantage of unsuspecting self-employed con-
sumers. In fact, they have been forbidden by the Insurance Com-
missioner to open any new accounts in Washington state. I keep
reminding myself that at least I am still here to deal with this, even
if I can't afford the interventions that saved me.

A month later, a letter arrives. Tucked in to a pile, it appears
to be like all the other medical paperwork that David systemati-
cally files in folders that thicken each week. Imagine our surprise
to find what I have miraculously been granted: *Eighty-five thousand dollars written off by the Northwest Hospital Foundation.* I am
left with a zero balance. Tears of gratitude well up in me. Relief.

Who is responsible for this? Who can I possibly thank? I call
the foundation to ask who to address a thank-you letter to, and
am told "the administration"—a faceless non-human entity to me.
The generosity composed of many individuals shares responsibility
for what has been gifted to me: to be spared in another way, this
time from financial collapse.

Missing in the mammoth pile of bills incurred through my
cardiac arrest and remodel, there haven't been any from the surgery clinic. I doubt that this is covered by the charity at Northwest that has so graciously covered my hospitalization. I perceive
the hand of Mary Scarlett behind this, and write to thank her for
easing the way, telling her that it has been challenging enough to
go through the physical side of arrest/surgery/hospitalization and
that I can't imagine adding bankruptcy to the mix.

I let her know that her caring presence helped ease the way
in allowing myself to be subjected to western medicine; how she
helped dispel my sense of the field of medicine being impersonal
as a result of its objectification. I share that her continuity of care

relieved my fear. How can I express my gratitude for her compassion, which has been priceless in my healing?

∾

*January, 2008*
*Seattle*

## New Composition

Recently Garima, a former student of mine, wrote from Germany to share a dream she had: " ... *You were actually COMPOSED anew of some unearthly substance. Have you been recreating yourself?*"

I tell her Yes! I am recreated day-by-day in rest and effort, in zest and progress. The slice of scars begins to heal over, a zig here, a zag there: a lightning bolt imprinted from my collarbone, between my breasts to below my ribcage; two small cross-shaped incisions from where tubes drained; the ragged slashes over my left pectoral muscle where my implanted defibrillator bulges. My lower left rib, which kept slipping out of place, stays put longer each time it is adjusted, providing a thoracic spaciousness that I am grateful for, uncramped.

My convalescence evolves. I increase the distance of daily walks at Green Lake. Two miles now! I teach a class, amazed at how much I love being in the classroom again. I begin to plan future work. Although I still need to pace myself, I find I have more fortitude than I have for years. What the doctor referred to as the "wicked" obstruction in my left ventricle outflow track is fixed from a significant gradient to practically zero. In other words, my newly adapted heart is working fine—well enough now to cut back on the killer medication, Amiodorone. My whole being lightens as the dosage decreases down to none. A liberation!

But there are other more insidious changes. At night, I awake weeping to be so irretrievably wired. The site where my defibrillator is wedged is inflamed. My body is trying to reject what it knows as foreign. In an X-ray, I see the contraption embedded in me with its crisscross of wires, its probes. I find I am unearthly in an entirely different way than Garima meant. I find that the deep throb and burn that pains me originates from the site where six wires cross. Dr. W's nurse advises Vicodin or high doses of Tylenol at the very least. I find the homeopathic remedy Hypericum/Arnica soothing enough to make it bearable. Still, nothing can assuage the distress of having become bionic, to have mechanization entwined in my physique.

David takes me for the first reading of my device. *Interrogation,* it is called. Over my shirt, a probe is positioned on top of the defibrillator. It transmits a signal to a machine called "Merlin." A record of my heart's electrical data is conveyed and printed out. What does the device reveal? Conferring with the "wizard," Dr. W sees that my heart's rhythm has remained fairly constant. He adjusts the controls of the device to function as a backup only when intervention is needed, instead of having it on all the time. The doctor says it is rare that a patient can feel the little kick of pacing. I have. What a relief to have my heart beat on its own.

But there are things that no device can tell us. After research and various consultations, my team of cardiac specialists agree: it would be most prudent not to recheck the defibrillator, since that would involve stopping my heart to see if the internal shock might start it again. *Might.*

We all remember that I nearly died the first time it was tested. It could be that my heart was overstressed so close to surgery and that it wouldn't necessarily happen again. But it is still high risk. Moreover, there is nothing they could change in the device I am stuck with. If it didn't work, we would just know it couldn't be depended upon.

This is a controversial issue among electrophysiologists. Here is the dilemma: *1) dying from my heart being stopped during a test, or, 2) dying from the device failing to work should I go into cardiac arrest once again.*

In the face of this, how do I compose myself? Weighing the odds, I elect not to have any more interventions. I would rather have my heart stop on its own than to be interfered with again.

All along, I have tried to follow my heart, not to respond out of fear. Having made this choice sets me free from the dread of going back into the bardos of going under again so soon. I have four to seven years until the battery runs down and the defibrillator will need to be exchanged. It's not simply a matter of battery replacement, but of a brand new device being installed. It will be attached to the remaining leads, which adhere to veins and heart tissue. Hopefully, I can avoid surgery until then. Hopefully, over time, I can make peace with this invited intruder.

෨

*Spring, 2009*
*Seattle*

## Tandava

Shiva takes poison everyday. So do I. His is snake venom; mine, rat poison, of a pharmaceutical grade. He takes his by letting a cobra, coiled about his neck, bite him, and through this becomes immune, invincible. I take mine in prescribed oval pills, to keep my blood stream from clotting dangerously.

It is the second spring since my surgery. I am leaving the coagulation clinic. My blood is out of its therapeutic range. My medication needs to be readjusted ... yet again. My steps echo down the dimly lit fire escape stairs. I almost stomp, wishing I could escape my blood. Walking out into the hesitant spring day, I almost cry. I head to the graveyard across the street and walk along the circular drive lined with budding cherry trees. Scent of wet earth wafts on gentle breezes, in an otherwise still place. New bouquets of tulips have been set on a cluster of graves in an old family plot, their limp red and yellow blooms fading. Across the grounds, on the other side of the hedge, is the crematory with its smokeless chimney.

Shiva has ash from the cremation grounds smeared over his bluish skin. He sits on Mount Kailash in samadhi, eyes closed, wearing cobras. These snakes are entwined about his head, neck, and arms as his hair cascades in massive dreadlocks, the Ganges river flowing from one, the crescent moon rising from another. In one hand he holds a three-pronged staff, in another, the *damaru*, an hourglass drum, from whose beat and rhythm language originates. His other hands are held in the mudras of protection and blessing.

I still feel tricked. I woke up from surgery to be told that a titanium valve had been sewn in between my heart's left ventricle and atrium. My old *whoosh* sound is replaced by a *clap* that is audible without a stethoscope. This dime-sized apparatus prevents my blood from slushing back and forth as it did before. Instead, it keeps going forward, beat by beat: a new phenomenon in my heart's physiology.

Having this mechanism embedded in my flesh brings risk. Without intervention, blood would instinctively congeal around the metal valve, to protect me from this intruder. I can't help but notice the medication to combat this is named Warfarin. This warfare taking place inside me is invisibly fighting clot formation—clots that could loosen and land anywhere in the thousands of miles of blood vessels that branch through my body. A clot that could cause an aneurism or stroke. In order to offset this possibility, Warfarin alters my blood's chemistry. The hope is to keep it in the right balance—thin enough not to clot, but thick enough to prevent a fatal bleed.

Shiva, as Nataraj, lord of the dance, is supremely poised, perched on the demon of ignorance, lifting one leg in a curve as he demi pliés. His many arms extend in all directions, one still holding the damaru drum, another holding a bloom of the whirling flames that surround him. He is engaged in the vigorous dance of Tandava—the rhythmic play of the universe, counterpoised between creation and dissolution.

There is no one else in the graveyard on this overcast morning. Only the dead. I've come to the newer graves—shiny marble, inscribed with decades I have lived through. I am glum with failure from this unexpected dip in my anti-coagulation. Until two weeks ago, I was stable for four months after a year of slowly increasing increments of my dose. I began with two milligrams; now I am up to twelve and back to weekly checks. Before this setback, I had settled into tracking my blood monthly. I put off traveling until last month, since it impacts the fine equilibrium between hemorrhage and thrombosis regulated by Warfarinzation. I changed my diet a bit—not advised. I didn't realize it would take me into such a low range.

As a heart patient, I have had to focus on what my parameters are between activity and rest, exertion and ease. No extremes. Now, a similar dynamic takes place on a cellular level within my blood. Regularity, rhythm, predictability, routine. These are keywords in guiding my daily life—eating the same foods day in and day out with the same amount of green each day; pacing myself to have times of activity offset by rest, safeguarding against overstress. I am on the quest to find a midpoint between viscosity and ooze, a constant reminder of balance. Shiva Nataraj, may I find your poise as I learn to master this! I know that where your dance takes place is not a distant mountain, nor a holy ashram, nor a sacred city, but the human heart.

In the distance, a siren blares and subsides as I continue to walk, passing a cherub of darkening stone—child hands enfolded in prayer.

လ

*Fall, 2008*
*Seattle*

## Transformative Trees

David has accompanied me to Northwest Hospital for my coagulation check, "just like the old days," when sternal precautions prevented me from driving myself. It's a year since my operation. Since it will be a ten-minute wait for my prescription to be filled, we decide to head over to the main hospital building across campus to say hello to the nurses on the telemetry ward, to look for Susan, especially, who invited us to stop by sometime to say hello.

As we enter the lobby, my body fills with foreboding, a visceral repulsion that spreads from the pit of my stomach. I halt and tell David that I am not ready to go upstairs. "Okay," he says, taking my hand. "What's going on?" How can I give words to this trembling, issuing from the depths, this wavering akin to dizziness that threatens to overwhelm me. I don't feel safe here. "I just can't go back." I tell him, squeezing his hand.

Then I notice the trees—four cardboard cutouts, each about ten feet tall, set up in the lobby against large windows. They sing with color. It is a display, "The Transformative Journey of Illness." I lead David by the hand, over to where we can read about it. Each tree marks a stage: Grief, Refuge, Allies, and What Has Changed. There is a description of the project and an invitation to name one's own experience of these phases by writing them on blank leaves to place them at the base of each bare-branched tree.

"Let's do this," I propose, leading him closer. "Sure, sweetheart," says David, as he leans in to hug me, adjusting to the fact that I am not willing, yet, to return to where I lay as a patient. I find comfort in the sturdy trunks and branches of these trees, this structure that names and gives voice to phases of illness. I take up a stubby pencil from the basket and, moving from one tree to another, write down what occurs to me on the maple-shaped paper leaves:

… for Grief I write: "the fragility of life" and place it by the first tree.

… for Refuge: "my beloved's embrace" joins the other cutout leaves on the floor.

In gratitude, I name my Allies: "spirit beings and my dear ones here who have seen me through," and place my leaf by the third tree.

When I come to What Has Changed? I pause, pondering: where to begin? There is a sense of gratitude for being here, for my life being given back to me. There is an opening to sensitivity for all those who suffer from disability and illness, but I write the most fundamental: "loss of trust," and add it to the other losses, by the last gnarled tree.

David has been standing nearby. I join him to look at photos of the participants who made these trees. These cancer patients are my unknown comrades—dealing with facing mortality, living with disease, having to integrate limitations into their lives. Later I will find out that this project was created by Melissa West, the wise and compassionate therapist that I have been working with to honor my own journey of dealing with the repercussions of my sudden death, to unclench anxiety's hold.

There are times—out of the blue—such as not being able to face the telemetry unit this morning, that my body lets me know what it wants, tense with "no." The first time, a month or so after surgery, I had not left home much, except for walks and medical appointments. My sternum was still healing, so I couldn't drive, and a colleague was giving me a ride home from a committee luncheon. We were driving in heavy traffic on the viaduct, high up. Unease overcame me, so startlingly that I had to grip on to—what? To keep from dissolving, rising up and away. The cars were too vivid in their steel and push, the road too dense, the day too glaring, the view too wide. On this edge of vertigo, what was there to hold on to, to hold me from spilling out?

Or other times in noisy restaurants, sitting still yet not finding stillness—porous to the cacophony of voices invading me, as
if the volume had been turned way up. Accompanying the clamor,
a mass of energies bombarding me. I was permeable, needing to
grasp on to something, anything, to keep from melting away from
the acute intensity of the unfiltered moment.

On this stark journey, no self-help books on returning from
sudden death, on confronting the enormity of that void. In this
realm, I grasp at goddesses.

Psyche's last task in serving Aphrodite (goddess of beauty,
goddess of love) is to fetch some of Persephone's beauty cream
from the Underworld. Impossible. Psyche chooses to hurl herself
from a tower instead, but its stones speak to her, telling her not to
abandon hope. The road that she is shown—between the upper
and under world—is untraveled, but she is given safe passage. She
has coins for the ferry man and barley cakes for the three-headed
guardian hound of hell. As instructed, Psyche resists assisting the
various souls that beg her for help, but stays on task. When she
arrives in the desolate palace, Psyche sits on the stone floor before
Persephone and partakes of simple bread instead of the magnificent meal offered to her. Persephone bestows a small canister of her
beauty to Psyche, which she has been warned by the tower not to
open. But when she makes it back to the land of the living, Psyche
wants to borrow a dab of that mysterious cream, assuming it won't
be noticed. The moment she lifts the lid just a crack, she is plummeted into oblivion. She wasn't rescued with electric paddles, but
by Eros shaking her awake. Only then does she become his bride.

There are times I strive to remember—where is it I went
when my heart stopped and so much effort was made to bring me

back? I begin to cascade towards an unsteadying brink, then stop short, a membrane enfolding me. Fear—a guardian that keeps me here.

When they hear of my brush with death, people often ask me: *Did you see a tunnel of white light? Did you meet spirits of your loved ones welcoming you?*—the typical near-death experiences. I've always been wealthy in my dream life, but have only a void to report. Silence is better suited to the place where Persephone was abducted against her will, to that somber depth she surrendered to and eventually becomes queen of. How do I contain that mysterious gift? Her beauty: oblivion. A beauty even Aphrodite (goddess of beauty herself) sought and required Psyche to fulfill.

Back in the upper world, I check my watch. "My prescription should be done now," I tell David as I lead him away from the lobby. We pause in front of the automatic glass doors to fasten up our jackets, bundling up against the autumn chill. Stepping out of the building that I was so restless to leave last autumn, I sigh, breathing deeply of the fresh air. I brace myself to walk into the wind.

ॐ

*Winter, 2008*
*Seattle*

## Being and Non-being

Strolling through *Garden and Cosmos*, an exhibit of centuries old watercolor paintings from courts of Jodhpur, I come upon one that utterly arrests me. Amid depictions of lush gardens and courtesans, this folio is an arm's-span wide, dramatically divided in half. On the left side: an ashram forest—holy men framed with caves of stylized mauve rocks, surrounded with paths and plants in an effulgence of hues. Trees in emerald and sage, fruits in rose pink and orange, flowers in lemon and mustard golds. A busy scene as a wise man gives counsel to a suffering king.

On the right side: a black void. Looking closer, one sees it is composed of thumb-sized, swirling curves of gold. I recognize it immediately: the blank I tried not to careen into during my sudden death and its aftermath. Vishnu sleeps on a serpent bed, fifteen heads curling to enfold him in a protective arc, as he floats in the milky ocean of dissolved existence. In absolute silence, he dreams the universe into being.

∽

*July, 2008*
*Seattle*

## Reclamation Ceremony

It is my fiftieth birthday, a shimmering, warm July evening—not too hot. Patti and I have walked over to Green Lake, to set up for a ceremony that I have invited a few friends to celebrate with me. There is a crowd with fold-out chairs and coolers spread out right by the trees that I had envisioned stepping around and through for the seven thresholds, to end with coming out from the mantle of green and passing through two birches that form a natural doorway. We'll have to improvise. I put down the heavy basket I am carrying and we look around.

We decide to set up right out in the open, down Oak Hill, with the seven thresholds marked in a line, ending close to the two birches. Although I would have preferred a secret garden, this is somehow the perfect place. Being out in the open with scores of people passing by is akin to the bustling airport where I collapsed.

While we wait, a lama in his maroon and gold passes by within six feet of us, his bare feet stepping firmly in the grass. I've seen him, accompanied by students, quite a few times in my circumambulations of the lake. He will pass back by later and nod to us again during the ceremony itself. It is Kenpo Rinpoche, the high lama who gave Laurie the transmission of the Medicine Buddha that she practiced with me during my hospitalization.

David and my friends arrive and we form a circle. I begin by sharing my intention for this Reclamation Ceremony. I want to enact, symbolically, healing from the intrusions, shocks and losses of surgery and to celebrate coming into being fifty—to invite full embodiment. I share what I've discovered—that *reclaim* means "to demand the restoration or return of; to call back." It is my hope that this ceremony will do so.

I acknowledge the ever-widening circles of loved ones, allies, angels and divine beings. I offer:

> *May the fruits of this ceremony be dedicated to all*
> *beings, especially those undergoing health crisis*
> *and surgeries.*

Then I read Merna's poem:

> *who really knows*
> *what's coming*
> *toward the heart*
> *the curve ball that will*
> *fling itself your way*

*we belong to what arrives*
*there's no catch*
*but the open hand* [6]

I continue, "When Inanna journeyed down to the Underworld, something was stripped from her at each gateway, until she entered the throne room of Erishkegel, naked and bowed low."

So did I.

Now I will journey back, reclaiming what was stripped away, earmarking certain thresholds. This ceremony represents a dynamic process, and some of these gateways are ones that I continue to meet. I ask for the gateways to be represented by two people holding up their arms, meeting to create an arc, London Bridge-style. I have invited each of them ahead of time to give me a particular gift that expresses the gift of reclaiming the element of the threshold they represent.

I begin with my body, the Earth element.

I acknowledge that my natal heart was formed lopsidedly, with spiraled cells rather than linear ones, which caused it to be enlarged and literally too open. Eventually this form couldn't sustain me and arrested. I chose radical interventions to reshape my heart's anatomy in order to function well. A trough was carved in my overly big left ventricle and a new valve—a "butterfly"—was inserted in my mitral leaflet.

*May I accept my physical limitations and be ever grateful*
*for the many forms that healing has taken in coming to*
*me, and continues to.*

I will carry this clay bowl through each gateway. It represents my physical body.

I come to the first threshold, the Threshold of Awareness, earmarked by a list of all the anesthesias and sedatives used during my hospital stay, too copious to invoke—and a *dorje*, for clear consciousness.

Numerous times, through anesthesia and sedation, my consciousness was interfered with, dimmed down and shut off from awareness. I experienced disturbing states of consciousness, bardos, between this world and others.

Laurie places the dorje into my bowl and a small *thanka* of the Medicine Buddha.

*I reclaim clarity and continuity of consciousness*

Laurie and David create an archway and I pass through.

I come to the second threshold, the Threshold of Breath, the Air element, earmarked by my trusty incentive spirometer and a bamboo flute.

Numerous times my breath was taken from me. I was given breath by a stranger. I was breathed by respirators and a heart-lung machine. My lungs collapsed during open heart surgery and were filled with fluid in a complication following heart surgery.

Holly holds a little pinwheel made of Japanese paper and hands me the flute.

*I reclaim my ability to breathe deeply and to know*
*true balance in my life.*

I play a scale on the flute, breathing deeply and sustaining a trill of notes.

Johanna and Patti create an archway and I pass through.

I come to the third threshold, the Threshold of Circulation, the Water element, with an extensive old IV hook-up: a multi-tubed apparatus, with four portals and clasps leading into a central tube, tapering off to a fine point.

Numerous times my circulation has been invaded and interfered with. From being catherized through my femoral artery, to having my blood diverted from my heart to flow through a machine, to losing blood and receiving transfusions, from David initially to unknown donors of platelets when my anti-coagulation went too far and I bled internally. I lost count of how many times my blood was drawn, and how many IV ports were put into me.

Patti gives me a clay container with a lid.

*I reclaim a sense of my bloodstream being contained within my body and a clear awareness of my boundaries.*

David and Robyn create an archway and I pass through.

I come to the fourth threshold, the Threshold of Electrical Conduction, the Fire element, marked by copper wire. The ICD I carry within me, embedded in my left front shoulder.

Numerous times, when my heart was stopped or quivering dangerously, it was shocked electrically to try to bring it back into a stable rhythm. I was shocked with increasing voltage, until my heart responded. Besides the burn marks that were left on my chest, I was left with the repercussions of having taken electrical currents into my body, ten times in all. Wires were connected to my heart to pace it after surgery and one of the victories I want to acknowledge is that my sinoatrial node was left intact. I have an embedded electronic lifesaver here in me, which offers me a rich opportunity to befriend technology.

David places a little copper hoop in my bowl.

*I reclaim the electrical currents generated in my own*
*heart and seek to befriend the device I carry with me*
*to jumpstart my heart if needed.*

Holly and Patti create an archway and I pass through.

I come to the fifth threshold, the Threshold of Security, ear-marked by a brass lion lock from India.

Numerous times since my cardiac arrest and undergoing sur-geries, waves of anxiety have arisen in me. The unequivocal vulner-ability of almost dying and of being a heart patient has brought up other times in my life, early on, of not being in trust.

I recognize the need to move from victim to creatively col-laborating with what has befallen me, and put my trust in spirit.

Johanna places the lion lock into my bowl.

*I reclaim a sense of calm-abiding and trust my*
*destiny, illuminated with wisdom.*

Laurie and Patti create an archway and I pass through.

I come to the sixth threshold, the Threshold of Interdepen-dence, earmarked by a peacock feather.

Numerous times since my cardiac arrest, there have been oc-casions in my healing that express interdependence. From people in the airport who stopped to assist me when I collapsed (and saved my life without any acknowledgement) to the prayers of loved ones near and far that encircled me as I underwent surger-ies, to all the helping hands and support in making it through. Then there are the medical interventions, taking medicines. There is a story from Central Asia that I recently was told of peacocks eating poison and turning it into life-giving nectar. This poison/nectar creates the vibrant colors of its plumage, and makes the bird plump and prosperous. Poison, fully ingested, is transmuted into beauty and radiant health.

Laurie steps up and places a peacock feather in my bowl.

*I reclaim interdependency and celebrate that I am
not entirely self-sufficient, as I once strived to be. I
offer gratitude for all the ways that life is connected
and for all my magnificent allies! I appreciate relying
upon the kingdom of mineral, animal, plant, human
and even the pharmaceutical!*

Everyone creates an archway together and I pass through.

I come to the seventh threshold, the Threshold of Embodiment/Inspirit-ment, earmarked by the twin birches. By this time, the picnickers have cleared away from where these two beloved trees stand, elegant and strong, so we move there. I stand on one side of the opening between them, and everyone else—all fifty years or older—stands on the other side.

Numerous times in my life as a whole, for various reasons, it wasn't safe to be in my body. In my cardiac arrest and surgeries, this precariousness was reinforced and reactivated. I've always directed gratitude to spirit, for being incarnated in flesh. Now I begin to experience the gratitude to flesh for being there for spirit to incarnate in. Less and less is there separation. I accept my body with its limitations and needs and celebrate its capacity to love and create in the physical world.

Robyn places a flower crown upon my head and invites me through the doorway of birch.

I enter into fifty with unity of spirit and body, in joy and juiciness!

I step through the gateway of birch, accompanied by great cheers.

Then one by one in a circle around me, my dear ones read the collaborative poem that friends have sent blessings for from near and far, welcoming me to my next decade. The sun is going low in the west, throwing golden light on our little hillside as a bluegrass duo plays nearby. The face of the lake is calm as people keep scurrying by. I embrace each of my beloved friends, smiling in delight as the blessings settle in.

❧

*Summer, 2008*
*Seattle*

## Dungarees

We are digging out old, wet ash from the sump pit discovered under the old furnace site when the basement floor was demolished. A crew of three worked for days breaking up the old gray slab of concrete and hauling it away. The broken chunks will be used for making new roads—somewhere. Our excavation site could be lunar soil, gray and dry, but it smells earth-musty. *Swoosh.* David is on his knees shoveling the black sludge into a bucket. While he fills another, I lug the first bucket and dump the sooty slush—*swoosh*—into the wheelbarrow that we recently assembled, part by part, together. This is new: that I am able to work alongside him, no longer only looking on and wishing I could join in.

Now that my heart remodel has been a success, we are re-building a part of our house—transforming an unfinished basement into a living space for my dad. He is ninety-two now, and eager to leave the retirement community outside DC, where my mom insisted they move. Then she died, leaving him stranded in a place he never would have chosen. We want him close by and couldn't find a house we could afford that would work for all of us, so we're converting this one.

David used to drive off to work, now he goes down the stairs. Every time he dons his work clothes and saddles on his tool belt, I admire him. His worn leather bag with the measuring tape clipped on; the pouch with its slots holding a charge tester; a side-cutter; a stripper; an assortment of pliers and drivers; electrical tape, dangling in rolls of four colors; and his razor knife. There is his drill in its own pouch in the back and his hammer that can be in a ring to his side when he's using it often, or behind him, hanging down like a tail. He's well-equipped.

I admire the way David straddles a ladder. His hands know by heart where to reach for whatever tool he may need. Yesterday, I watched him cut into a wall with his Sawz-all, then bring out the wires from where they lay coiled in a box. He unwound them to see how the old knob and tube wiring runs—red: hot, and black: cold. He excels at tinkering, at figuring out how to put things together, his acute awareness of details honed in on mechanics. His precision is an asset in his trade—one wrong move could result in voltage unleashed: fatal shock.

Recently, we were shopping for socks and came upon a display of Carhartt work clothes for women—a new line. David's eyes lit up. "Let's get you a pair, for Christmas! What color would you like?" I eagerly tried on two sizes to find which fit best, and he bought them for me then and there to celebrate strength returned. I donned my work pants for the first time this morning. Heavy brown canvas, double-kneed—stiff in their newness. I look forward to their fading as his pair has, over time. He digs deeper and I heave old ash, clearing the space to create a new foundation.

~

*Fall, 2008*
*Seattle*

## New Configurations

I am back at the school where I teach. This morning I was here in this familiar room with students in a simple circle of chairs. Tonight I've returned to find it crowded with all manner of props. Huckleberry Hall has become a laboratory. There are tables with various models of shapes and even a clear cylinder of water four feet tall. The white-bearded geometrician brims with enthusiasm to demonstrate his process—ten years of intensive research through art and experimentation that has led to his discovery of a new form that correlates to the human heart.

Surfaces, dimensions, planes, properties and proportions, ratio and relations in space. The word "geometry" is derived from *geo* – earth (Gaia) + *metreia* – to measure: a study of the form of Gaia. Projective geometry extends this to map the invisible. The audience is aglow with curiosity as we take in what this wizard has to show of the heart's dynamic configurations. We try to follow his fathoming of the relationship of spirit and form; how it is all about transformation and measuring movement as a static structure; how it all starts with root three—beyond measurement; how the heart has seven edges that correlate to a shape created from three pentagrams whirling, how seven is the first number of chaos, how the heart sits at a forty-five degree angle but root three of its placement reveals more. This former sculptor shows us the process of inversion—turning a shape inside out continuously, and how inverting a cube reveals an ovoid; that inverting a tetrahedron/ octahedron (was it?) results in a seven-sided form with nine golden proportions unfolding into stars; that this shape is akin to a bell when it is spun. A Grail unveiled.

Although I certainly can't follow the precise progression that comes to completion with a double heart, I find resonance. I am spellbound as I listen. I avidly scribble notations that are only cursory: That blood is the consistency of milk; that the heart fills spiraling clockwise and empties spiraling counter-clockwise—two vortexes: one curve accelerates and one decelerates—two spirals coming together in opposite directions with no clash; that the apex of the heart is paper thin, so if it was merely a pump, it would bulge there; that rotating the heart just five degrees would result in a new valve being formed. A fifth chamber—a new dimension to antici-pate as we evolve beyond the anatomy we possess today. Perhaps my cardiac malformation is simply a precursor to a new cardiac form?

∽☙

*November, 2008*
*Seattle*

## Facing Mutation

The plump phlebotomist with a bleached perm reaches out for the papers I am handing her. "Marge" is embroidered in blue script on her lab coat. I tell her that I am here for a blood draw to be sent out for research. She is flustered. "We can't do this!" she snaps.

Corey, the genetic counselor, had warned us that it wouldn't fit into the lab's system and gave us her phone number "in case it's a problem." It is. David gives Marge the number to call. Disgruntled, she picks up the phone. There is no code on the lab's form for what we are requesting. She asks us to take a seat and calls her supervisor in. She shares her cubicle with a cutesy stuffed animal, a descendent of a Care Bear, no doubt. Across from us, fish swim in a bubbling tank. Blues and yellows glide gracefully through undulating green. We wait. After a conversation in hushed tones, I am called back up to her booth. The only way they can handle it is to do it as a "courtesy draw."

A vial of my blood is being sent on dry ice across the country to Correlagen Laboratories, in Massachusetts. Only later do I realize that my ancestors on both sides dwelled there. The laboratory will attempt to isolate the mutation responsible for my heart defect. There is a seventy percent chance that they will be able to identify the culprit, an autosomal dominant disorder. It may have been stamped into my genetic code from my ancestry or it may originate with me. There is a fifty percent chance that this phenotype, or trait, will be passed on to my offspring. If the gene is successfully isolated in me, the next step will be to test my children to see what is enfolded in their DNA. Are their cardiac cells penetrated with disarray? Will it carry on in the hereditary stream and take expression in my progeny?

Inwardly, I growl at the possibility. Mother bear. But this is a predator I can't fight or defy. Passing on this genetic twist goes counter to the core gesture of motherhood—to keep my dear ones safe. It is one thing to deal with being impaired myself, but to consider a legacy of damage plunges me into despair. The perfectionist in me is outraged. How dare I impart this imprint? As if it is my fault: this flawed design of cardiac cellular disarray.

﹏

Summer extends and the equinox passes as I wait for the test results. The weeks they had predicted become months and there is still no word. This autumn, a year after my cardiac arrest, I am grateful to be outside in wind and sun, in rain and leaf fall. I remember how last October, I watched trees change through the hospital window. Now, on an overly-warm day for this time of year, I ride a bike for the first time in years. I pedal and glide in the park near my home. I am in fine shape, increasing my activity week by week. There is still the sting of the wire stitches in my sternum, and an ache if I press the down too hard on the handlebars, but I mostly feel better than I have in years.

*Except for this foreboding: that what is entrenched in me will be passed on.*

After riding a bit, I stop to sit at the lake's edge, and lay my bike down. At the sandy beach where I took my children to play summer after summer, I sit under a willow tree. Gazing across the softly rippling water, I consider one of the key principles in homeopathy—*miasm*, the inherited susceptibility to certain diseases. Genetic testing is a quantifiable expression of what Hahnemann (the founder of homeopathy) defined as a predisposition, an invisible disease imprint on an energetic level that transmits its influence to subsequent generations. For instance, someone whose parents or grandparents had tuberculosis may have weaker lungs. In my family, it's a damaged heart. Here in modernity, all has become narrowed to what can be measured. Having spent so much of my life attempting to live soulfully, I may very well be remembered for what will be left stamped in flesh. The irony of it stuns me.

I have grieved for humanity in a general way. Now sorrow stabs me personally: my blood line, endangered through what may be engendered through me. Pondering future generations coincided with my first heart symptoms during the Council of All Beings, my wounding vision of archetypal suffering, of nature being harmed. Fifteen years later, the seasons are askew and dangers I sensed in foreboding have come—are coming—to pass. This unseasonably warm day, for instance, just one of many extremes of weather that are becoming commonplace.

There is a Buddhist teaching that, when one takes a cup of salt and puts it in a cup of water, that it is impossible to drink; but when one dilutes the same cup of salt in a pristine lake, it is perfectly fine to partake of. I look across the green waters, knowing this water is not potable, but I like the image anyway.

Grief. How do I find the right dilution?

Tears flow. I accept the cold facts, the "putative genes," the pathogenesis that I carry. I know that their orchestration originates beyond conscious choice. But this hereditary stream that my life flows in is only one in a larger confluence.

Knowing my life will eventually become husk, I contemplate the ancestors who have seeded me. Here, a presence I have often sensed through my life—my paternal grandmother. Her love was imprinted into my being, as formative as any physicality. That grace continues to inform me. Her spirit guardianship opens to ranks of others: mothers, angels, guides so close, so tangible.

The mandala I envisioned in facing my surgery spontaneously encircles me.

The knot of grief in me loosens, expands beyond miasm to another stream. Rivulets emerge from a deeper source, radiant with the absolute privilege of being here on Earth, in time, embodied, even in a body with a warp in the spiral of DNA. How can I enrich this invisible cloak and hand it down along with the loam that will be the matrix of my descendents?

A seal set upon their hearts.

⁓

A few days after my cry at the lake, Rose and I are doing the dishes after supper. As she reaches out to throw something away in the compost, I catch a flash of color on the back of her left arm.

"Rose … is that a tattoo?" I ask as I reach for her.

"I knew you would hate it!" she exclaims, yanking her arm away from my grasp.

She is right.

When she lifts her sleeve up all the way to show me, I look closer at her imprint: four black skulls on a cross, eyes gaping. It is this Guns N' Roses icon she has chosen to celebrate the freedom of turning eighteen, instead of the original images she designed over the years—of roses and snakes curling in the arches of her feet. She always was intrigued by Hades. Is this her marking of the Underworld? It's the permanency that alarms me. No regard for the future.

At least she hasn't chosen extreme body piercing. Almost all of her friends have tattoos, some are tattoo artists. She was in love with a young man who underwent scarification. In tones of admiration, she's told me of the ritual involved, a rite of passage like the sun dancers' of the Sioux, where wooden pegs are run through the skin on the dancers chests as they dance in trance for days and nights. I read this as a cry for deeper feeling. Rose and her good friend Echo cooed over my fresh scars after surgery, admiring how "cool" they were. Are.

Scars as beauty? I smear vitamin E and comfrey ointment on my incisions, hoping they will fade, as if it's possible to not leave a trace. As if that severing of flesh didn't make its mark.

I am still reeling from Rose's choice of new expression—her tattoo—the next day when I hear back from Corey, the genetic counselor. I am sitting in my office when she calls, apologetic for the delay, and cheery with the results of my DNA sequencing. Three sarcomeric mutations have been isolated. She reminds me that to have something show up is good news. By fax, I receive the highly technical test results and a study published by the American College of Cardiologists from the Mayo Clinic entitled, "Myosin Binding Protein C Mutations and Compound Heterozygosity in Hypertrophic Cardiomyopathy."

The report from Correlagen Laboratories, a "Multiple Gene Evaluation," is carefully worded as uncertainty is emphasized, "possible pathogenic sequence variant"

MYBPC3, MYH7, TNNT2.

"Genetic counseling is recommended. A concordance study of variants and disease within the patient's family may clarify the variant interpretation." But the Mayo Clinic study establishes it clearly: I have the most common "putative HCM-causing defect" pointing to later onset, as well as one associated with more severe forms of the disease.

These mutations are a warp in the binding of proteins, re-sulting in ineffectual contraction on a cellular level of the cardiac muscles—the sarcomere. In dyslexic French, sarcomere could be *sacre mère*, evoking Sacred Mother, Sacred Sea. Our Lady of Salty Waters.

Weeks later, David and I meet again with the genetic re-search team at the UW Medical Center. We crowd into a window-less room with the counselor, Dr. J, the geneticist, and the research fellow who is eight months pregnant. I wonder if she has fears for her unborn one, focused as she is on heredity. Corey brings an extra chair in and we all sit down. After laying out the results, Dr. J explains that a sarcomeric mutation means that there is a change in an amino acid in the cells of the contractile tissue of the heart. "Not folded in as nicely" is how she puts it.

The bottom line is that what has shown up in my testing is very likely to be disease-causing and it would behoove us to have my brother and children checked. Now that they know what to look for, the testing is straightforward and less expensive. If my mutation shows up in them it doesn't mean that they will neces-sarily manifest HCM symptoms. If they are clear of the mutation, then they will no longer need to be screened by echoes every few years. The main point that is dwelled upon in this three-hundred-plus dollar meeting is that if my family members do opt for test-ing, they will no longer be eligible for life insurance or disability insurance. Marked for life.

A few days later, I call the nurse coordinator of the HCMA Center of Excellence at Stanford. It's been over a year since I was in contact with them. Before I say much, Heidi has my file on her screen and recognizes my case. She is willing to work with the whole family. She tells me that since my children are of childbearing age, if they do carry the sarcomeric mutation, when they want children, they will have a choice to do a "PGD"—a pre-genetic diagnosis. She explains the procedure: after in-vitro fertilization, with sixteen eggs harvested from the hyper-ovulated mom, mixed with "daddy's sample" in a petri dish, they test the embryos that form for pathogenic variants and choose an unflawed one to return to "mom," to embed.

I say "thank you" and hang up, haunted.

I wouldn't be here to worry about this Brave New World scenario if my parents had been given the same choices. Although it is a rearrangement of my own making, more whimsical then DNA being fiddled with, I call on *Sacre Mère*—Sacred Mother.

*May my children and theirs be free of this mis-weaving in flesh.*
*May the scars of my progeny be as superficial as tattoos.*

꩜

*Spring, 2009*
*Seattle*

## Beyond Reptilian Brain

After a little trip with David to British Columbia, I confess to Patti that I couldn't sleep most of the time and I am resistant to going away again. She recognizes that I am exhibiting symptoms of post-traumatic stress. Below where words reside, there is the residue of my arrest and its repercussions: multiple shocks, literally and figuratively. I learn that the impacts of trauma have been mapped out and can be traveled with a guide. In a series of sessions, Robin

Shapiro, an expert in EMDR (Eye Movement Desensitization and Reprocessing) teaches me that my nervous system can't differentiate between then and now, when stimulated by certain triggers. For example, my reptilian brain equates leaving home with dying.

In time, I learn to clear those vestiges of terror by confronting them, and letting go. Robin provides safe haven by being present, offering perspective. Tactile pulsers in my hands thrum, alternating between my right palm, left palm, right, again and again, predictable. Charioteer holding these high-tech reins, I see the irony that the rhythm they bring is electrical, a redemption of the paddles that convulsed me numerous times. As Robin directs my attention to re-experience that moment, I let my sudden death arise in all its vivid alarm. The pulse throbs from palm to palm and I watch a point of focus in the here and now. My body shakes in primal release, shuddering as it lets go of all the fear harbored so instinctually. I discover how hard I fought to stay here and that the danger has passed. I re-encounter angelic presence that was present even then alongside the panic. Gradually, the remnants of anxiety wash away and dissolve.

Eventually, I will venture forth again.

☙

## Ode to My Implantable Cardiac Defibrillator

Unwanted child, bulge in my flesh,
Pest in my pectoral,
My collarbone's cumbersome intruder—

You resemble a cell phone
securely sewn in.
Screwed to my heart, blind.

Wizard circuitry binds us
slick intervention
Threaded through my veins

Finely calibrated lightening
Poised to strike
if need be

If I need you

May I move from gripe
to gracing you:

My darling device;
My reader of rhythms,
My counter of beats
Ally, back up—
Regulator, stabilizer,
Pulse I can count on

May I find tenderness
in our high tech
interdependence,

May our bionic bond be blessed.

*Spring, 2009*
*Seattle*

## Day-lighted

Water bubbles up in the midst of the stream bed and spreads in rivulets, sparkling in the afternoon sun. I am at the spot across from Northgate Mall where five years ago Annie, Francie, and I grieved the imprisoned waters. For over fifty years, this creek flowed in a pipe, unseen, unheard beneath concrete. Now it glides in a shimmer of light—and flows on.

I stand still on the bank by newly planted ferns and welcome this return, this freeing of the waters. Impossible to revert to the original riparian zone, this is a revision—a new stream bed, a "bioswale"—carefully engineered to incorporate the filtering of storm water. Cattails rise from the murmuring stream, alongside slough sedge, rushes and reeds. Native plants that once grew wild are tame here, carefully cultivated to purify toxins. A couple of yards from the source, water tumbles down a wall of stone—runoff from the streets. The interstate roars nearby. On average, 187,000 cars pass through this watershed every day. We are surrounded by human habitation. Hardscape.

Across the footbridge, a young woman sits on the only bench, sewing in the sun. I can't tell what she is stitching. Following the stream as it curves through the development, I explore. Concrete, steel, and glass engird this meander. For the last two years, this city block was off-limits. I watched from afar through the construction fences. Dug down. Built up. Now I seem to have it to myself. Condos and apartment units on one side—Thornton Place and Aljoya, upscale "retirement living" on the other. Packed in. The place is empty, a ghost town in reverse. There are a few orange SOLD signs pasted to windows, but it is as yet unpopulated. In time it will be abuzz with residents no doubt, but it was completed just as the housing market tanked.

Time will tell if this new "green" neighborhood design will be a success—units built for urban living, high density, boasting of proximity to a transit center, bike parking, energy and water efficiency, extra insulation, low VOC interiors, and one thousand tons of construction waste, recycled. This new urbanism is a far cry from cedar canoes, the first technology that interacted with this marshy place. There are some small cedar seedlings, planted on a bank.

Cedar trees once served as a sacred resource to the Duwamish who lived here, and they traditionally used its bark to make bedding, mats, tinder, torches, nets, sails, bandages, hats, clothing, imbricated baskets and boxes. They used limbs of cedar to scour fishnets and cut planks for longhouses, and carved it into masks, totem poles, paddles. Now the mall, looming just across the street, replaces cedar as source of provisions. Commodities.

I consider Grandmother Cedar, who once offered me refuge in my dreambody vision. She would be amazed at my non-indigenous body now, with its own feat of engineering, as compromised as this wetland. Thornton Creek's restoration is not a return to its original state, before myriad degradations. Nor is my heart's fix a return to how I once was, before I was cut open. Before being wired and implanted with this cumbersome bulge, tucked in just beneath the skin under my collarbone; before having a titanium valve clicking clock-like in place of my mitral valve; before having to track my blood's thick and thin; before I became aware, viscerally, that any moment could spell exit.

But here, in my rejoined and rejoicing heart I remain acutely awake to the astonishing grace of being here. I walk amidst the dual rushes of traffic and water, of bloodstream and breath, of Gaia and Sophia, Earth and spirit. My defibrillator is poised to shock away any threat of dysrhythmia, its microprocessor programmed to intervene. This is the symmetry I have befriended—angels on one hand, high tech on the other—my version of wholeness and holiness, after all.

✑

*Autumn, 2012*
*Seattle*

## Haywire

The trickster continues to insinuate himself into my heart's journey towards healing. Sometimes he whispers: *Things are not always as they appear!* Other times he declares: *Beware!* What was invented to be of help turns out, in some cases, to bring harm: I have recently discovered that I am one of 128,000 heart patients endangered by a defect connected to the electrical "leads" of my St. Jude's internal defibrillator.

"Externalization" it is called: the insulation in the lead has been found to deteriorate. Abrasion causes the wires to poke through the sheaths that enclose them. This can result in giving electrical shocks to patients the device is meant to protect. There are also record numbers of short-circuiting, with the same outcome. Help becomes harm, and many have died as a result. Anyone with an internal defibrillator will tell you: no lifting of weights, no reaching above the shoulder. I avoid crunching my left shoulder in sleep. I swim a one-sided stroke. I have no symmetry in my sun salutation. But the danger of damaging the wires, through kink and fray, has never been so overt.

The week that the recall was announced, David and I met with a technician from St. Jude's for a complicated adjustment to my device. I used the opportunity to ask about the recall (unrelated to the reason for our meeting), and was met with smooth talk and party line, downplaying the danger. Was he following the same script that I heard when I called the company for information a few days earlier? Months later, the New York Times Business Section ran a piece about the controversy over St. Jude's lack of disclosure about the malfunctions, highlighting the continuing issue of safety in the ten-billion dollar heart device industry.

I've played with names to forge a more personal relationship with my "safety" device. "ICD" is too abstract. At first, I tried "Bionica" to invite the possibility of character, but that appellation didn't adhere. Over the years, "Zapper" arose more naturally from David. Lately, though, we've slipped into referring to my "IED" jokingly—my own personal internal explosive device, an exaggeration of the internal danger that looms. Oh, it could be worse!

At first, most doctors advocated extraction of the faulty leads, but that procedure tears heart tissue or leaves broken pieces of the wire inside veins. When removals resulted in a high percentage of fatalities, the FDA published a recommendation against doing so. Precautions for me take the form of bi-monthly "interrogations" (instead of once a year). I have been given my very own "Housecall," a remote monitor for my ICD meant to operate over my phone line that hasn't always worked. These sessions leave me

drained and irritable, inexplicably zapped of energy. Despite re-
peated attempts, I can't get through to anyone to have St. Jude's
pay the extra expense for these additional ICD interrogations, at
five hundred plus, a shot.

I haven't received any shocks yet, for help or harm. The latest reading of my "zapper" shows, as expected, that the battery is
running low. The defibrillator will need to be replaced soon, connected to the dubious leads embedded in me. This means undergoing the same surgery where, last time, my heart was stopped
deliberately and almost didn't respond to being shocked back
into working.

Not something that I am eager to undergo.

The original announcement about the recall from HCMA
advised "a thoughtful conversation with your personal doctor
to choose the correct path for *you*." Physician opinions differ.
Case-by-case clinical decisions are being made, weighing risk
factors and odds. I have a choice in how to proceed. My path is
not straightforward. Has it ever been? Facing this dilemma demands becoming informed: to investigate options, seek second
opinions, consult with allies, both visible and invisible. I will
feel frustrated, powerless, insecure, afraid. I will question. I will
weep. I will pray. Ultimately, I hope to trust the navigation of
my heart, rooted in deep wisdom and open to grace, in whatever
form it takes.

❧

*Autumn, 2012*
*Seattle*

## Wounding's Grace

Sunshine slants low across the horizon. Phone in hand, I gaze out at the evening sky as my dear friend—my sapphire sister—shares the result of her uterine biopsy with me. I listen as she finds words:

> on one hand:
> terror;
> and on the other:
> an acute awareness of the utter preciousness of life ...

In this dual urgency, she shares the tender vulnerability of being rent out of complacency into the supreme sumptuousness of being alive. We both serve Tikkun Olam, the healing of the world through sacred story, through poetry, through teaching. We gather the shattered pieces to once again contain the holy light, and lo and behold, we are the ones being shattered.

As her fragile and courageous voice comes over the phone line, the phrase "Wounding's Grace" comes back to me—an epithet, a kenning, my code for this heart's journey, for hers, for others faced with suffering. I try to tell her how the depth of grace corresponds to the depth of wounding, that illness can be undertaken as an initiation, in whatever guise it comes in. I have seen this grace at work in those close to me as they have struggled with kidney disease, with breast cancer, with rheumatoid arthritis, with prostate cancer, with hepatitis C, with ovarian cancer, with a shattered hand. Each of these friends in their own way has found/is finding acceptance of their own version of brokenness and embrace.

I recall my experience of dropping into sheer emptiness, and yet being held by angels and ancestors—

> on one hand:
> mortality,
> on the other:
> a glimpse beyond ...

To know, side by side, preciousness and precariousness; privilege and edge; tranquility and terriculament. To know the divine ground that holds the void, as we move forward in the absolute wonder of each breath. Lamentations from depth of wounding, praises from depth of grace.

Our heads know that crisis equals opportunity, that the heroine's journey includes descent. In suffering the shards, we get to practice it. Let me be an ally as she faces this illness, this healing— to partake of what others meet every day with fewer resources. Let her be shielded from the assault of that dread word of her diagnosis, and all that adheres to it in fear. Let me invoke the muse of inexplicable paradox, to recreate this illness in her own way, on her own terms, inclusive of grace. Let me remind her, remind myself, of the words of Novalis:

> *To love is always*
> *to feel the opening*
> *to hold the wound*
> *always open.*

And may Isis enfold her, enfold us, as our journeys continue ...

> *Arise in us*
> *Bride of Osiris!*
> *For your way is as torn*

*as His holy green;*
*His body hacked and divided*
*cast*
*to the many cornered world.*

*But all corners round*
*soothed by your tears—*
*smooth each jagged edge—*

*Let your rivers flow.*

*Rekindle the tattered search*
*to gather his shattered green*

*One by one*
*Each scattered piece*
*Reclaim.*

*Arise in us*
*Bride of Osiris!*
*Morning star: Awaken*
*and descend —*
*Enfold us*
*In your great and gracious wings.*

To end:

Silence, to which all words return.

# AFTERWORD

I am accustomed to writing introductions, and have written quite a few. Introducing a book, I feel, is the art of opening a door and ushering in the very soul essence that someone has brought to life through the gift of writing—in such a way that the life is enhanced even more.

But with Mary Oak's writing it seemed that saying anything before encountering the experience itself would risk fostering the mind-set of narrative consciousness at the very moment one is about to enter into something akin to hearing a musical work.

The author and Lee Nichol, the editor of this book, collaborated very closely to find the best way to assist a reader in going through an experience rather than just having one. Mary has brought a new form into being, and it is, as the very title of the book suggests, a musical form. Mary told me once that the musical form of the oratorio historically enters at almost the same time as the opera. The difference is that the oratorio inherently retains the sacred character of the story, while opera is secular. Opera, of course, can be about sacred matters, but I am speaking here of the very structure of these two forms. Here, we are invited to enter an oratorio rather than an opera.

This distinction leads us into an afterword, with the purpose of re-sounding the verve, the enthusiasm, the particular sacred quality of this story. For indeed, this is a sacred story, and one that has the power of re-linking (religio) us with the fullness of what it is to be human. While this story is individual, it goes so deep that it is also a universal human story. It bursts through in its telling, disturbing us, throwing us out of a sleepiness and a denial regarding suffering that has cast the illusion over the world that suffering is "bad" and must be eradicated. That kind of progressive humanistic view leads to the projection of suffering onto the world, everywhere and senselessly, because we, individually, no longer have the capacity to bear it, nor to see that in bearing it, something of inestimable value is born.

The mind jumps in immediately, countering with its premature conclusion that no one, absolutely no one, would dare, in this progressive age, condone suffering. But this mind is in collusion with a long culture of scientific and technological humanism, and is sorely out of touch with human nature and the fullness of purpose of human life. Only half a story is told by the "eradication" imagination. The very first awakening occurring through this book is a restoration of the wholeness of our nature.

The ego-argument is also erased by the story itself, for in Mary's story, there is the living through of suffering, but certainly no hint whatsoever of the seeking of suffering. That inherent and living difference is what makes this telling so significant. In addition, the sacredness reveals itself not in the content of the story per se, but in the way the content speaks. We feel *with* the author, not *for* the author.

The avoidance of self-centered emotion and the most careful telling of a story through the larger context of feeling makes possible experiencing the most excruciating suffering without a drop of self-pity. Instead, what actually occurs in the reading is a gradual but unmistakable awakening of the spiritual realm of feeling—in the very sense of the word itself—to touch, as in "to feel" something, to touch someone. In this instance, feeling here feels the soul of another as one's own. The result is total and complete affirmation, even joy, in what our author has experienced. Notwithstanding the mind's objection to being put in such an awkward position as to actually affirm that there is value in suffering, we feel this truth down to our very core in what Mary has given us. We do not pity her—we feel, with her, the truth of being expandingly human.

Suffering without consciousness differs enormously from suffering that has found its proper mode of consciousness. In the extreme—an extreme that, alas, is presently put forth as the proper desire—suffering without consciousness is simply denial. Louis Lavelle, a great writer on the problem of evil and suffering, said that the worst misery is not to be aware of misery. Next to this pathology, there is suffering, that, while strongly felt, still has no psychic element—it simply hurts, and the psychic element is placed into the fantasy of escape. In this sacred story that Mary tells, there is the hurting, no doubt about that—over and over and over again. And through this seeming repetition, which is not repetition at all, we experience an inexplicable deepening—of who Mary is becoming, and thus who we can potentially become.

Deepening always indicates soul, the very expression of spirit as clothed and taking its destined course through the world. No anesthetizing here! Instead, we participate in a long series of visits to Hades, Inanna, Persephone, where the soul's imagining of inevitable suffering is located. What we learn through participating in this imagination is not that there is value in suffering, but rather than suffering is the very source of valuing; not valuing life, but the valuing of the mystery of embodying as Earth beings—where life and death exist, every moment, simultaneously. That is the reality of being human. We lose our humanness the very moment we split these apart, taking death as only an inevitable future rather than an actual present. Every moment we are living, we are dying.

Many readers perhaps feel twinges of the perverted form of Christianity that, for a long time—and with great damage— seemed to say that it is good to suffer, and in fact inflicted a great deal of it on individuals and on the larger world. Because of that perversion, a great secret, a great mystery central to a true Christian imagination, has been bypassed. When Christ died, the story goes that he descended into the depths of hell—we might say, the very depths of suffering. There are no stories or imaginations of what happened there. And because we do not hear what happened, we tend to miss what is most apparent—the descent into hell indicates that hell has been sanctified. Similar stories of the sanctification of the underworld occur in Mayan mythology too. Oh, my goodness! It does not take the "hell" out of hell, but it means, at a soul level, and even at an ego level, that our suffering is sanctified—as long as we do it, and minimize thinking about it and all that wants to pour in to try and negate the inherent valuing that is created through the experience.

Do not take this drawing attention to the missing element in stories of Christ as a religious pronouncement as much as a way of imagining the inherent source of value in suffering. It is as if a whole darker half of our human nature holds the very key to joy where one least expects it. With a caveat, of course: forget the Good Friday suffering and the Sunday morning resurrection joy imagination. The fantasy of "Yes, there is the bitterness of winter, but then that makes possible the spring," the "Well, I suffered so much, but I got so much out of it" fantasy. The valuing of suffering is not the after-view once we are out of it. Only imaginal pictures, stories—like the many stories Mary tells—can convey the inherent source of valuing in suffering. Concentrating, contemplating, meditating on the many stories in this book, reading them through over and over, not skimming or looking for answers to why this "poor" person had to endure such pain—only then does this marvelous book truly turn into a guide book, a path through the depths that have no bottom.

No transformation fantasy, please. Transformation is a very tricky word, almost as tricky as the word "healing." We tend to take soul words and try to baptize them into literalness. As a soul word, transformation means death as a perspective, as a way of seeing, of being present, really present; it is the way of dying, and only human beings can be conscious of dying—of relinquishing something every moment. Not arriving at the other side of dying. None of us know the other side. Those who find the art of suffering are perhaps closer, and are our most near mystics. That realization is perhaps the joy of this book, not the egotism of suffering that would say, "Hey, this is worth doing, look where it gets me." There is transformation—transforming into a religious being, becoming capable of creating a religion of one's own, from the creative core, one without any dogmas.

Another aspect, crucial, of what Mary gives us—there is a science of suffering and that science is patience. Indeed, suffering often turns us into a patient, one with enduring patience. The word "patience" suggests passivity, a kind of waiting without stirring and without hope. Rather, patience is *highly active waiting*, not for something to happen, but the art of waiting that awakens the life of the soul, and it does so in every cell of the body. Hope is present, and no longer confused with wish, for hope inheres within suffering and is not some add-on virtue that one is supposed, sometimes, to derive from having suffered. With this realization, the short psychological history of soul—depth psychology—meets its nemesis too, for depth psychology (certainly that of Jung) and even archetypal psychology, insist that soul is not body. That is not what we experience in this writing. Rather, we feel the "psychic" body forming, we feel the body now forming into an organ ... of compassionate presence.

The really amazing quality of this book is that it is impossible to put down. It seems to be about needing to know what will happen next. It is actually soul's joy in being re-discovered. Here we have something that, if you look at the content alone, is horrendous. But, something else is happening. An invisible process happens through the story—the author is becoming a religious being. Not someone who has a religion or clings to a religion, but discovers that to be human is to *be* rather than to have religion. That is, we find the link with the divine (religio) in our embodiment, and in particular, embodiment "in extremis."

I want to touch on yet another aspect of what Mary has written, again something that is not spoken about, but is in the very nature of the writing itself. This book, first by its words, but also by its very existence, circulating in the world, is testimony to the fact that suffering completes its meaning when shared—shared in the exact "right" way, not just spilled out. A picture of "the right way," which you will immediately see is the way of this book, has an archetypal background in the Greek story by Sophocles, *Philoctetes.*

Philoctetes, on the way to Troy with Agamemnon and Menelaus, got off the ship at the tiny island of Chryse to sacrifice to the local gods. As he was walking up to the shrine, he was bitten on the foot by a viper, a bite that immediately became infected. Black and festering, it was soon a raging, bleeding sore. Pus and rot attracted maggots to the wound, filling the air with a stench that no man could stomach. His companions, nauseous from the sight and smell of the wound, took him from Chryse and left him on a deserted island. There was nothing on that island—no trees, no plants, no animals—only the dry earth and rock crags. Philoctetes would not have survived except for the bow and arrow given to him by Heracles. Heracles had received the bow from Apollo himself and had given it to Philoctetes when he was dying, for Philoctetes had served him by lighting his funeral pyre. It was a remarkable instrument, that bow. It never missed the mark, such was its precision. Though few were the birds flying overhead, he never missed a shot and life was thus barely possible.

For ten years all there was on that island of suffering was Philoctetes, his maggot-ridden, never-healing foot, and a dead bird to eat from time to time. Filled with bitterness and rage, isolated and lonely, Philoctetes gave up on humankind and gods alike. Then, one day a ship comes to the shore. Two figures leave and step onto the island. One of them is Odysseus, and the other, a young man—Neoptolemus, son of Achilles. They have come to retrieve Philoctetes, for an oracle said that Troy could be conquered only with the help of Philoctetes and his bow. The plan is to trick him into coming with them. When Neoptolemus meets and talks with Philoctetes, he finds he cannot trick him. He admires the courage he sees; he waits with Philoctetes, hears his stories, cares for him. Odysseus, watching from afar, finally enters and threatens to force Philoctetes to leave. Philoctetes grabs his bow and is about to shoot Odysseus when suddenly Heracles appears in a vision, telling Philoctetes that he must go to Troy.

On the island, Philoctetes turns against the gods and all humans for this bitter injustice. He says to himself: "Necessity has taught me little by little to suffer and be patient." Being patient, paradoxically, means forgetting one's connections—with others, with the gods, with a typical sense of hope itself. And, in suffering, one is removed from the community of others; suffering is the only reality. No one is there to say what is happening, why it is happening, what brought it, where it is going. When we suffer, the explanations, the happy prognoses, the encouragement of those around, while comforting, also sound hollow. The name "Philoctetes" means "love of possessions." I do not know if this individual had many possessions, but now he is not even in possession of himself. He no longer belongs to himself, he belongs to suffering. And what occurs in the place of suffering is the birth of imagination!

André Gide's modern version of this Greek drama illustrates this aspect clearly. Gide's Philoctetes says:

> My images, since I have been alone, so that nothing, not even suffering, disturbs them, have taken a subtle course which sometimes I can hardly follow. I have come to know more of the secrets of life than my masters had ever revealed to me. And I took to telling stories of my sufferings ... I came to understand that words inevitably become more beautiful from the moment they are no longer put together in response to the demands of others.

We find this very sense of the free imagination of words as we read this amazing work Mary has wrought. There is an unmistakable sense that through suffering, imagination comes to prominence, and that true imagination is never private, not when lived; in and as the center of life, it is always community. Without imagination, suffering is blind necessity, with its attendant aloneness and utter isolation. But imagination has to come to us through inspiration embodied in community. It is not something done solely out of our own efforts. And, imagination brings something new to speech, to writing. It makes possible moving into the imaginal fabric of words themselves rather than just using words to convey information. Truth comes to expression. Community is healed.

Something of the ultimate secret of suffering is revealed in this book. It is, again, nothing stated as content, but the wonder one experiences in encountering this writing signals that the form of writing has indeed gone beyond itself in what is conveyed. The secret is this: Can we imagine God is a suffering God? Can we imagine that the very essence of the divine is suffering? A competing thought says "No! God is Love, not suffering." Can you tell the difference between the two in this writing? I cannot. But, it is a different aspect of God than that given in theology, certainly, and even in most mystical revelations and spirituality. To get this, though, takes entering into this writing deeply, and with powers of imagination as something very real, not imagination as the relief of the "unreal" in times of oppression, or simply our everyday escapism. When we encounter suffering that goes as deep as that of our author, we see that it is met with all the expected reactions, like fear, even terror. We also feel that suffering is a meeting with something else, not "elsewhere," but within the suffering itself—something holy beyond comprehension.

This introduction to veiled but strongly felt divine Presence changed Mary Oak thoroughly. Reading resonates with divine Presence that entwines with the very flow of this writing, and is enough to change one's life completely. We can even begin to notice and track what the changes are. They are "ideals" becoming lived, bodied realities. Courage, honor, faith, encouragement, ennoblement, pride, compassion, self-sacrifice, happiness, passion, affection, magnanimity, authenticity, decency, hope, gentleness, civility, conviction, community, steadfastness, ingenuity, liberty, responsibility, friendship, prudence, tact. Are not these the qualities that pervade this writing? Qualities that have not been learned through academic schooling, qualities that are lost in the culture, qualities that are in fact more or less derided in these times, but here, in this book, they live and are embodied as the outflow of the encounter with suffering. They are qualities that in fact can never be lived by knowing *about* them—they then remain only ideals, and in this completely greed-oriented culture, they are not even ideals any longer.

What we discover through empathetic reading is that these seemingly outmoded "virtues" are actually not—nor have they ever been—of our doing. That is, we, on our own, well, maybe we can develop them as kinds of cultural virtues, meaning "codes of conduct" to live by. They are powerful enough that mindful contact with them can have this result. In this writing, however, we sense that such qualities are in fact the way that soul embodies through the process of entering suffering with strong awareness. These "virtues" are what happens when necessity is encountered, met, lived deeply, neither rejected nor judged. It is as if suffering is the passageway flowing between necessity and imaginal reality. By "imaginal reality" I mean qualities that are actually present, bodily present, that are "here" and "not here" at the same time. This imaginal dimension used to be the realm of myth. The best definition of myth I ever heard, paraphrased here, comes from Mircea Eleade: *myth is something that never happened but is always happening.* That is the way with these qualities brought into being through the passageway of suffering. It is perhaps not necessary to name them, though the purpose in doing so is to help give contours to the feeling dimension that is so prevalent in Mary Oak's *Heart's Oratorio.*

To further the contour, then, we can name the ways in which the depths of the feeling dimensions are entered, such that embodied, living ideals issue from them: complete surrender (we cannot *do* this, we can only get to the point of letting it happen); letting go of guilt, grieving, individualizing—yes, at all costs, even when "trapped" in "the system," taking that imprisonment as the opportunity of discovering how individuality can never be eradicated; maintaining good boundaries, even militantly; avoiding politicization; getting comfortable with vulnerability, fighting on, with humor; bringing out the best in people; not *having* faith, but *living* faith!

Robert Sardello, Ph.D.
December, 2012

# NOTES

1  Seed, John; Macy, Joanna; Flemming, Pat. *Thinking Like a Mountain: Towards a Council of All Beings.* Philadelphia: New Society Publishers, 1998.

2  Thank you to Suhrawardi Gebel for sharing his version of the story used in the production of *Sajecho: Voice of the Earth.*

3  Rilke, Rainer Maria. *Sonnets to Orpheus.* M.D. Herter, trans. New York and London: W. W. Norton Publishing, 1992. (Sonnet 2:2)

4  Hyde, Lewis. *Trickster Makes This World: Mischief, Myth and Art.* New York: North Point Press, 1998. (All italicized passages in this section are drawn from this book.)

5  Levertov, Denise. "Growth of a Poet," in *Poems, 1972-1982.* New York: New Directions Publishing, 2001

6  Merna Hecht, original untitled poem.

# Glossary

**Abode of the Message:** a residential and retreat community of the Sufi Order of the West, founded by Pir Vilayat Kahn in 1975 in New Lebanon, New York on four hundred acres of beautiful land that was formerly the Mount Lebanon South Family Shaker Village.

**Anthroposophy:** the philosophy developed by Rudolf Steiner in the early part of the 20th century which literally means "the wisdom of the human being." Steiner defined Anthroposophy as "a road to knowledge leading the spiritual part of the human being to the spirit of the universe."

**Anthroposophists:** those who devote their lives to the practice of Anthroposophy, sometimes lovingly referred to as "anthropops."

**Anthroposophical Medicine:** developed in the 1920s by Dr. Rudolf Steiner and Dr. Ita Wegman, based on an integrated image of the human being as a whole, including physical and metaphysical dimensions.

**Archangel Michael:** an archangelic being of courage.

**Artemis:** Greek virgin goddess of the moon and the wild whose arrows bring illness or healing to women.

**Arrhythmia:** an irregular heart rhythm, too fast (tachycardia) or too slow (bradycardia), that if sustained can become dangerous.

**Atrium** (singular), **Atria** (plural): the top chambers of the heart that fill with blood while the ventricles are contracting.

**Atrial fibrillation:** a common arrhythmia where the atria lose their normal contraction pattern, resulting in an arrhythmia.

**Bodhisattva:** an enlightened being who is committed to the complete liberation of all living beings.

**Cardiac arrest:** the sudden, unexpected loss of heart function, breathing, and consciousness, usually resulting from an electrical disturbance in the heart. Compare this to a heart attack, which is the common terminology for an acute myocardial infarction due to atherosclerosis and coronary heart disease, which blocks blood flow to a portion of the heart.

**Cardioversion:** a method to restore an abnormal heart rhythm back to normal by using an energy shock delivered to the heart. This shock briefly stops all electrical activity of the heart and then allows the normal heart rhythm to return.

**Curative Eurythmy:** a therapy developed by Rudolf Steiner and Dr. Ita Wegman, MD as a part of Anthroposophical Medicine, prescribing movements to work therapeutically on the etheric or subtle energy body.

**Dreambody:** in Process Oriented Psychology, the "dreambody" is the mirror connection between our nighttime dreams and our body experiences. Every dream refers to, or "mirrors," a particular body experience, and every body experience can be visualized and may appear in dreams."

**Gaia:** Greek goddess of the Earth. In contemporary ecological movement, used to signify the living Earth.

**Heart failure:** a weakening of the heart, rendering it unable to perform the work necessary to keep up with the body's needs. In most cases, heart failure is accompanied by significant fluid accumulation in the lungs.

**Homeopathy:** a system of medicine that uses the law of similars ("like cures like") and attenuated substances to stimulate the human being to heal. The AMA was founded as a direct attack on homeopathic institutions.

**Hypertrophic cardiomyopathy:** a congenital heart disease characterized by a thickening of the left ventricle that can lead to obstruction of circulation and electrical instability. HCM occurs in 1 out of 500 people, but often goes undiagnosed. For a great resource on HCM, see the informative website of the Hypertrophic Cardiomyopathy Association—an advocacy and patient support organization: *www.hcma.org*.

**ICD:** implantable cardiac defibrillator—a device that is surgically wired to the heart; it automatically senses and terminates lethal disturbances of heart rhythm via electrical shock. In addition, it can be set to intervene by pacing the heart when arrhythmias occur.

**Isis:** ancient Egyptian heavenly mother goddess who is often depicted with outstretched wings.

**Mandala:** a visual tool that connects and focuses the unconscious mind on the symbolic world. A mandala is circular and often represents the interconnectedness of relationships and wholeness. It can be oriented towards healing.

**Mystery School:** centers of initiation (such as Eleusis in ancient Greece) that were secretive and provided spiritual training of individuals in prescribed ways.

**NIH:** National Institutes for Health, a government-funded research institute that did a clinical research on HCM for over forty years as a part of the National Heart, Blood, and Lung Institute. Its HCM Clinic closed in 2003.

**Padma Dakini:** Tibetan Buddhist female deity who burns away passion and attachment to find the wisdom of discriminating awareness.

**Potentization:** the process used in homeopathy and Anthroposophical medicine to release the potential of a substance from its physical matrix to increase its energetic force.

**Process Oriented Psychology:** developed by Dr. Arnold Mindell for working with physical symptoms and psychological processes as two mutually interdependent aspects of a large and more comprehensive system, which he calls the "dreambody." The model has roots in Jungian psychology, quantum physics, and shamanism. Over more than three decades, it has been refined and extended into the fields of psychiatry, interpersonal relationships, large group process, and work with serious physical illness.

**Raphael:** archangelic being of healing.

**Rosicrucians:** a mystical Christian sect that sought to integrate the sacredness of science, art, and religion. Upon invitation of William Penn, a hermitage was established by Johannes Kelpius beside

Wissahickon Creek in Philadelphia in 1694, after Kelpius and his followers had been persecuted in Germany.

**Septal myectomy:** an open-heart surgery that removes a small amount of muscle from the upper part of the septum to eliminate mitral valve leakage, resulting in pressures within the heart to be within a normal range.

**Sinoatrial (SA) node:** the biological conductor of electrical impulses of the heart.

**Sinus rhythm:** the normal beating of the heart, as measured by an electrocardiogram (EKG).

**Sophia:** goddess of wisdom. In Gnostic Christianity, Sophia is understood as the feminine form of the godhead, the holy spirit within the human being.

**Subtle bodies:** the invisible energetic fields that surround the physical body.

**Sudden death:** the most devastating and unpredictable complication of HCM. It occurs without warning signs from lethal heart rhythm disturbances (called ventricular tachycardia and ventricular fibrillation).

**Sufi meditation:** drawing from many mystical traditions, includes practices with light, sound, and identification with transcendent divine attributes.

**Sufi Order of the West:** founded in Geneva, Switzerland in 1910 by Hazrat Inayat Khan, a classical Indian musician, focusing on the unity of religious ideals and love, harmony and beauty. This path of mysticism is considered to be "the path of the heart."

**Tara:** Tibetan Buddhist female bodhisattva of compassion.

**Quakerism:** also known as the "Religious Society of Friends," this Christian denomination honors simplicity and peacemaking, places one's own relationship to the divine as paramount, and worships in silence.

**Ventricles:** the two lower chambers of the heart that squeeze blood into the lungs and aorta.

**Ventricular fibrillation:** a life-threatening arrhythmia consisting of rapid and premature repetitive beats within the ventricles.

# ACKNOWLEDGEMENTS

No writer exists in isolation. I bow to those who have made it possible for me to pursue taking up this story and to those who have helped midwife it into being. How can I possibly give thanks for the many ways in which this creative work has been nourished? I hope that my sense of gratitude has been evident in these pages.

Foremost, for the heartfelt presence of spirit guardians.

I bow to those who have mentored me in this process. Nancy Mellon, with her sensitivity to healing story, has provided heartening witness to my journey in all its storied forms. Randy Morris provided true guidance as my advisor at Antioch and opened doors to Mythopoetics and Sacred Ecology. I am indebted to working with the heart imaginatively from the work of Robert and Cheryl Sardello in Spiritual Psychology, beginning with a workshop on the Broken Heart and continuing with their interest, as Goldenstone Press, in sharing my story. Deep bow to true encouragement! Terry Tempest Williams, exemplar of *rubedo*, whose passionate insistence that I tell my story ignited my will to do so.

I am thankful for the MFA program in Creative Writing at Antioch University, Los Angeles, where my final manuscript of "Ecomythic Memoir" contained a portion of what evolved into *Heart's Oratorio*. Sharman Apt Russell sustained sentence sensibility and Brenda Miller was a key influence in paring down to essence. I was also fortunate to have Brenda provide a manuscript review and pruning of the greatly expanded version, post-MFA.

I bow to those who provided invaluable feedback in reading over various drafts at different stages of my book-in-becoming: Karen K. Lewis for her insight and vital comments, Patti Pitcher with her unflinching honesty, Waverly Fitzgerald with her grounding of vision in mercurial know-how, Annie Blampied with her soulful gaze, Cesca Diebschlag with her astuteness and enthusiasm, Janis Craft with her sensitivity as a playwright to rhythm, Kim Scanlon with her musical illuminations, Judith Gille with her practical clarity. Each of these women is engaged in her own creative pursuit that I find truly inspiring. I am honored to accompany them, as they have accompanied me.

I am thankful for Dorothy Craig's alchemical edits. Lee Nichol of Goldenstone Press provided editorial positivity, from the whole down to the detail. A truly Jupiterean holding!

Thank you to Eva Leong Casey for cover and interior design.

I bow to the circle of dear ones, family and friends, who have accompanied me in this journey of stoutness and grace. My dear friends, Geraldine and Ayesha, who both passed on in the course of my writing this. Thank you to my spectacularly loving kids: Christopher, Emmanuel, Kyrian, and Rose, who have each respected my writing pursuit over the years. I am indebted to my father, Louis, for his exemplary rhythm and routine as he writes his memoir (at age ninety five!), and to my brother Niles, whose warm humor offers a needed balance to my gravity.

In addition, I want to voice my thanks for my teaching colleagues on the faculty of Sound Circle Center for respecting this other work of mine alongside our shared endeavor to transform our culture through arts and re-envisioning education. I am also grateful for my students who continually inspire me with the power of creativity. Most of all, none of this would have been possible without the grounding of love provided by steadfast sweetheart and partner in grace, David.

### A Note on Naming, a Passage on Permissions

In completing *Heart's Oratorio*, it was invaluable to run what I had written by each of the physicians involved, to check for accuracy and gain permission. For the most part, I found them, although a couple had retired. My depictions were met with interest and enthusiasm by each of them, and yes: permission. The only exception to this was one cardiology clinic that "cannot approve use of our legal names in the text, either personal or corporate." Any physician whose name is reduced to a single letter is either part of the clinic that cannot be named or was not reachable. Inclusion of a full last name indicates that they have consented.

The most notable consequences to my seeking out permissions are that Dr. McKenna is following up on research using my medical records and Dr. Fananapazir asked for my forgiveness in the way he treated me.

Therapists and friends have also had an opportunity to approve my renderings. My first husband, Atum, declined reading the manuscript, but gave permission to be named, based on his respect for my perspective. Of course, his version would be different.

~

Thanks to New Society Publishers for permission to reproduce excerpts from *Thinking Like a Mountain: Towards a Council of All Beings* by John Seed, Joanna Macy, Pat Flemming. Philadelphia, 1998.

Thanks to North Point Press for permission to reproduce excerpts from *Trickster Makes This World: Mischief, Myth and Art* by Lewis Hyde. New York, 1998.

"Remodel" was first published in the journal *Anesthesiology Today.*

"Murmuring" was first published as "His Heartbeat" in *Heartscapes,* Kate Harper and Leon Marasco, eds., Plainfield, Vermont: Spruce Mountain Press, 2012.

# ABOUT THE AUTHOR

Mary Oak's work is rooted in a love for the living Earth and a spirituality that draws from many sources. She is on the core faculty of Sound Circle Center in Seattle, where she teaches creative writing, storytelling, and nature awareness. She also works one-on-one as a writing guide.

Mary holds a degree in Mythopoetics and Sacred Ecology, and an MFA in Creative Writing, both from Antioch University. She is a seventh-generation homeopath, working in a wide range of healing modalities. One of her deepest joys is having raised three sons and a daughter. She lives with her husband, David Fries, in Seattle.

You may contact Mary at www.maryoak.com.

Made in the USA
Charleston, SC
29 September 2013